THE [illegible]
[illegible]

NOTES

including

- *Introduction*
- *Synopses*
- *List of Characters*
- *Summaries and Commentaries*
- *Review Questions and Essay Topics*
- *Selected Bibliography*

by
George F. Willison

INCORPORATED
LINCOLN, NEBRASKA 68501

Editor

Gary Carey, M.A.
University of Colorado

Consulting Editor

James L. Roberts, Ph.D.
Department of English
University of Nebraska

ISBN 0-8220-1030-5

Cliffs Notes, Inc. Lincoln, Nebraska

CONTENTS

Introduction

LIFE AND BACKGROUND

John Bunyan (1628-1688), an evangelical Baptist preacher, would have been forgotten long ago if he had not written *The Pilgrim's Progress,* which brought him fame and some fortune as a man of letters. The exact date of his birth is not known. But on November 22, 1628, no doubt as an infant only a few days old, he was christened in the Church of England chapel at Elstow, an old and tiny hamlet in Bedfordshire, which lies in south-central England, then a quiet and rather isolated countryside of broad cultivated fields and gently rolling wooded hills.

The Bunyans, an old family in the neighborhood, probably of Norman descent, lived about a mile from Elstow, down a country lane known as Bunyan's End because the family's cottage was the last habitation on the dead-end lane. Adjoining the old, thatch-roofed cottage, occupied by Bunyans for generations, was a workshop housing a forge, for the elder Bunyan was a tinker by trade, a maker and mender of pots and pans and other such utensils. Though requiring some skill, the tinker's trade was not highly regarded, largely for social reasons, the chief being that most tinkering at the time was done by bands of wandering gypsies, who were not socially acceptable. Competition with them was demeaning. Besides, the gypsies by taking whatever they could get for doing a job drove down the price of wares and services.

Bunyan later made out that he had been born and brought up in the poorest and most abject circumstances. But that was an exaggeration, a way of dramatizing his rise to eminence from humble beginnings. His father's tinkering provided the family with a small but adequate living, supplemented as it was by produce from a small farm—vegetables from the kitchen garden; fruit and berries from an orchard; eggs and fowl from the chickenyard; milk, butter, and cheese from a cow or two in the barn; ham, bacon, chops, fat-back, and lard from a few porkers in the piggery. In season, there were fish to be caught in the River Ouse and tributary streams and, occasionally, the family enjoyed venison, hares, or game birds from hunting in neighboring fields and woods. Nor did the Bunyans have any rent to pay for their farm. They were freeholders, owning their property, which had been in the family for generations.

As young Bunyan grew older, he learned the tinker's trade, helping his father in the workshop and going with him as he pushed his small wooden two-wheeled cart around the countryside to peddle his wares and services. Frequently, they pushed a few miles beyond Elstow to Bedford, the county seat, or shire town. Though it was only a village of less than a thousand people, Bedford was the metropolis of the area, the marketplace where farmers brought in their produce to sell and then went buying necessaries, perhaps even a few fripperies in the shops, no doubt after having enjoyed an ale or two in a tavern. The sights, sounds, and excitements of Bedford, small and unsophisticated as the village was, impressed the country youth from Bunyan's End.

As he went about as an itinerant peddler, first with his father and then by himself, Bunyan met and talked with people of many kinds, sharply observed the countryside and its ways—observations that he stored in his memory and found very useful when he came to write. He could call upon his memory for graphic details of scene, character, and conversation.

Somewhere in the rather lonely countryside, young Bunyan got some schooling. Not much, but at least he learned to read and write. This he always accounted one of his greatest blessings. At a time when schooling of any kind was usually beyond the reach of the poor, when most Englishmen were illiterate, the ability to read and write was indeed a blessing and opened a whole new world to Bunyan.

As a young man, he was addicted to reading what he came to regard as light literature, liking ballads, "a news-book," and adventure stories handed down from the Middle Ages. He liked particularly the story about St. George and the Dragon, and another about the simply incredible exploits of the legendary St. Bevis of Southampton in slaying monsters, fiends, devils, and assorted villains by the hundreds, always managing a hairbreadth escape from apparently hopeless situations. These and other popular medieval romances, with plenty of blood and thunder, provided exciting and heady reading for youngsters, and for the older, too. In their day they served what today is served by our so-called comic books starring such heroes as Superman, Batman, and other incredibles.

Bunyan grew up in a time of trouble, of bitter and bloody conflict, of civil war, with Parliament arrayed against King Charles I for his high-handed unconstitutional rule, with the religious Dissenters (Independents, Presbyterians, Baptists, Quakers, and others) arrayed against the official tax-supported church, the Church of England. By law, everybody had to belong to that church and take communion in it at least three times a year. All other forms of worship were prohibited; many thousands of people—Bunyan would later become one of them—were jailed or given even worse punishment for defying the law.

In 1642, when Bunyan was fourteen years old, fighting broke out in the Great Rebellion, or the Puritan Revolution as it is also known. Parliamentary armies commanded by Oliver Cromwell and others were soon chasing the king's forces around the kingdom, smashing them with great slaughter at the Battle of Marston Moor, where, said Cromwell, "God made them as stubble before our swords." The following year, in 1645, came the execution of Archbishop William Laud (who was "anti-Christ" to the Puritans) and the overthrow of the entire Church of England establishment with its special privileges and restrictive practices. Later, King Charles I was beheaded for "treason." When the House of Lords objected to these proceedings, that house was abolished, and the House of Commons proclaimed England a Commonwealth, with Oliver Cromwell, a staunch Puritan, ruling as Protector. From 1645 on, the Puritan spirit, shared by Bunyan and all the Dissenters, governed and dominated England for fifteen years.

In 1644, as a youth of sixteen, Bunyan had volunteered for, or had been conscripted into, the Parliamentary army and was assigned to a garrison at Newport Pagnell, some fifteen miles from home. He was never in combat during the war. After three years in the army, he was discharged, returned home, resumed his trade as a tinker, and soon married.

Not much—not even her name—is known about his wife except that she came from "a godly family," was piously inclined, and brought as her complete dowry a Bible and two religious books. The young couple took a small cottage and set up housekeeping with not so much "as a dish or a spoon betwixt us both," said Bunyan later. No doubt he was speaking metaphorically, but certainly they were very poor. It was a heavy blow and a continuing sorrow to them that Mary, the first of their four children, was born blind. After the death of his wife about ten years later, Bunyan remarried. The only thing we know about his second bride is that her name was Elizabeth, but as Bunyan always gratefully acknowledged, she proved to be a great comfort and source of strength to him during the long years he lay in prison.

But, so far, this biographical sketch has dealt only with the "outward man," a term Bunyan often used. A sketch of the "inward man" reveals more about the author, his nature, his problems, and how he came by a tortuous and torturing route to the main line of his life. At the age of ten or thereabouts, as he himself tells us in *Grace Abounding*, an autobiographical work, Bunyan became seriously worried about the state of his soul. When playing with youngsters on the Elstow village green, he would suddenly stop in the middle of the game to wonder whether he was sinning in so enjoying himself. Should he not have his mind on more serious things, such as saving his soul? Yes, he decided.

He gave up playing games; he stopped swearing. He had always greatly liked pulling the ropes that rang the bells in the steeple of the Elstow church. He gave up that, but bell-ringing still had such attractions for him that he would go with young friends and watch them pulling the ropes that set the belfry sounding. He was uneasy about this, however. Fearing a bell might be dropped on him for being involved in sin, he would crouch under a large beam for protection. But as a falling bell might break the beam and crush him, he decided to watch and listen from the steeple door. But he soon came there no more: "How if the steeple itself should fall?"

As Bunyan grew into adolescence, he fell into spells of extreme depression, as many adolescents do. He was obsessed with doubts, fears, and nameless anxieties. Certain that he was a great sinner, he was weighed down by an overwhelming sense of guilt. Earlier, he had often had terrifying nightmares in which he was being stalked by horrible monsters and by Satan himself pinching his flesh and jabbing at him with his pitchfork. Young Bunyan would wake up screaming in utter terror.

Now, under the pressure of increasingly severe emotional and psychic strain, his mind and senses became somewhat disordered. He began to have hallucinations. He would see the face of Christ in the sky and "the wrath of God in the very clouds," and hear voices calling to him from above: "Wilt thou leave thy sins and go to Heaven, or have thy sins and to Hell?"

Bunyan wanted to go to Heaven, of course, but he did not know the way and kept asking himself, "What shall I do? What shall I do!"—a desperate exclamation he later put in the mouth of Christian when he came to write *Pilgrim's Progress.* He was haunted by John Calvin's doctrine of predestination which underlay the beliefs of most nonconformist creeds. By that doctrine, most people were doomed from birth to end in Hell, no matter what they did on earth. Relatively few were predestined to be the "chosen," to be of the Elect who would go to Heaven to enjoy eternal life and all the glories there. This raised a most perplexing and disturbing problem—how to know whether one was doomed or of the Elect? In his distraught condition, Bunyan all but persuaded himself that he was of the doomed even though he was "in a flame to find the way to heaven and glory."

From 1647, when he came home from the army at the age of nineteen and married, Bunyan lived some six years in extreme inner torment. This period ended when he came under the influence of an accomplished nonconformist minister, the Reverend John Gifford, who had gathered together a small Baptist congregation in Bedford. Patiently, the pastor talked with Bunyan, explained the awful mysteries of the Faith, dispelled his doubts and fears, and assured him that he was doubtless of the Elect. After years of anguish, Bunyan was now at peace with himself—and with God, he hoped.

Along the way, he had been helped by chancing to come upon an old battered copy of *Commentary on the Galatians* by Martin Luther, "that stubborn monk" who had precipitated the Reformation in 1517 by nailing his ninety-five theses to the door of Wittenberg castle church in bold defiance of the pope, then both the spiritual and temporal overlord of western Christendom. Bunyan had long been wanting to read "some ancient godly man's experience," and Luther's *Commentary* was a godsend. "Excepting the Holy Bible," he said, "I do prefer this book.... before all the books that ever I have seen as most fit for a wounded conscience."

In 1653, renouncing the Church of England in which he had been baptized, Bunyan joined Gifford's congregation and was re-baptized in the waters of the River Ouse, which flows through Bedford. The congregation welcomed Bunyan, not yet twenty-five, as a most promising young member. He was soon preaching—at first privately, then publicly—for Bunyan discovered to his surprise, and to the inspiration of his listeners, that he had a command of words and style, that his mind sparked with vivid imagery, that he had a very moving eloquence because everything he said came so plainly from the heart.

With his conversion, Bunyan moved his family from the Elstow cottage to one in Bedford. He continued his tinker's trade, but found time to preach to religious groups in outlying places when invited, which was often, for his name was soon known all over Bedfordshire. He also found time to begin writing. His published works at this period, all in the form of pamphlets, included *A Few Sighs from Hell* and *Some Truths Opened*, tracts that were probably expansions of sermons he had preached.

For seven years all went well, until 1660, when the Puritan regime collapsed, the monarchy was restored, King Charles II returned from exile to ascend the throne occupied by his father and grandfather, the Church of England was reestablished, and everything possible was undertaken to eliminate or at least drastically reduce the influence of the Puritan nonconformist spirit that had dominated England for almost two decades, ever since the early 1640's.

While in exile, hoping to gain the support of the less radical Nonconformists, Charles had issued the Declaration of Breda to the effect that during his reign, if and when he was restored to the throne, no man would be molested because of his religious beliefs so long as he did not disturb the peace. The king was not a bigot, as his father and grandfather had been. Indeed, "the Merry Monarch" was interested in religion only as a means of keeping civil order. But the king was forced to break his pledge under the pressure of his Cavalier supporters in Parliament. Nonconformists had taken the lead in one great revolution, and they might attempt another, it was feared. They should be suppressed. A law passed in the reign of Elizabeth I was dug up, a new Act of Uniformity was passed, prohibiting the holding of nonconformist religious meetings and requiring all to belong to the Church of England and attend its services at least three times a year.

Nonconformists of all creeds apprehensively watched the storm gathering, and Bunyan was advised that, as the most prominent nonconformist preacher in Bedfordshire and likely to be the first struck there, it might be well if he suspended preaching and kept out of sight for a time. Saying that he would not run away because that would set a bad example, Bunyan went on preaching till late in 1660, when he was seized while addressing a meeting in a farmhouse not far from Bedford.

Brought to trial in the county court at Bedford, Bunyan was charged with "devilishly and perniciously abstaining from coming to Church to hear Divine services, for being a common upholder of several unlawful meetings and conventicles, to the great disturbance and distraction of the good subjects of this kingdom." Bunyan did not deny that he had been holding religious meetings, or that he had abstained from attending Church of England services. Several of the magistrates, rather sympathetic toward Bunyan, offered him a way out: he would not be prosecuted if he would promise "to call the people no more together," and go home and stay quiet. That would be against his conscience, replied Bunyan, and he was thereupon convicted and hauled away, at the age of thirty-two, to be locked up in the Bedford county jail for twelve years. His wife and others made repeated attempts to obtain his release, but to no avail.

The Bedford jail was like all English jails of the day, and long after —a stink hole, foul and filthy almost beyond belief. The stench in the prisons was so nauseating and overpowering that those coming to visit doused their handkerchiefs with turpentine and held them tight against the nose. There were no sanitation facilities except the most primitive. The only source of water was the hand pump in the prison yard. The food was meager, monotonous, unwholesome. Men and women prisoners were herded together, without privacy of any kind. All slept on straw, usually without a bedstead to keep it off the hard floor. Bedford prison had no fireplace so that it was freezing in winter. In summer, it was steaming hot because it had only a few small windows to let in a little light and air. Prisons were frequently swept by dread jail fever, which often carried off half the inmates. A long jail sentence at the time amounted, as often as not, to a death sentence. That Bunyan survived his long prison ordeal testifies to the health and strength of both his body and spirit—and to his good luck, too, though Bunyan ascribed his survival to the direct intervention of God.

The first turning-point in Bunyan's life had come when he became friends with the Reverend Gifford and joined the Bedford meeting. The second came with his imprisonment, which turned out to be the most creative period of his life. With the prisoners herded together, living in two large but overcrowded rooms, Bunyan could not hope for any seclusion. People were around him day and night. But he managed to live a quiet, fruitful inner life by withdrawing within himself to be alone with his feelings, thoughts, fancies. Or he could turn to reading the Bible both for solace and to improve his mastery of Holy Script.

Many of his fellow prisoners were Nonconformists, suffering, as he was, for their religious beliefs. At their invitation, Bunyan was soon preaching to this group, not only on Sundays but on weekdays as well. It is ironic that the jailer allowed inside the prison services that were not allowed outside, and for participating in which the prisoners had been jailed. Bunyan preached extemporaneously, never from a prepared script and seldom from notes. He would take a text from the Bible and "fly off" with it to the admiration and content of his listeners. When he thought one of his sermons was superior or particularly timely, Bunyan would set it down on paper before he forgot what he had said. A number of these sermons he enlarged and had published under such titles as *Christian Behavior; I Will Pray with the Spirit;* and *A Mapp of Salvation and Damnation.*

Bunyan also had longer and more ambitious works in hand during these years of confinement, finding plenty of leisure to think and write. It was an enforced leisure, to be sure, but it was nevertheless leisure such as he had never experienced when he was out in the world with its daily cares. The prison routine freed his mind "to study Christ," said Bunyan, who more than once rather happily described himself as "the Lord's free prisoner," having the time to do the things he most wanted to do without interruption. During his prison years, Bunyan completed several books and saw them published: *Prison Meditations; The Holy City;* and *Grace Abounding to the Chief of Sinners.* The last was a graphic and, at times, most extravagant account of Bunyan's physical, mental, and spiritual anguish before he saw the Light and was converted. Bunyan also conceived the idea of *Pilgrim's Progress* and began writing on it. But it was not completed by the time he was released from prison in 1672.

Bunyan and thousands of other prisoners throughout the kingdom owed their release to a proclamation by Charles II annulling all penal statutes against Nonconformists, and against Roman Catholics as well. Not that the king had become more favorably disposed toward Nonconformists, merely that he was using them to further his secret design of returning England to the Church of Rome, from which it had broken a century and a half before. Such a return would have been anathema to all Dissenters. But they knew nothing about the king's deep design. All they knew was that the penal laws against them had been annulled, and they were happy. Bunyan was so pleased that he published a tract in high praise of the king.

Returning home, not much the worse for wear after almost twelve years in a noisome prison, delighted to be once again with his family and friends, Bunyan did not resume his tinker's trade, for his Baptist brethren of the Bedford meeting had called him "to the pastoral office or eldership." Bunyan would spend the rest of his days as a pastor, conscientiously fulfilling the duties of his office, preaching and writing. His renown as a preacher, aided by his growing reputation as a writer, had now spread far and wide. Bunyan was invited to address congregations in neighboring counties, even being invited to London to preach to large congregations there.

For the Dissenters, things again took a turn for the worse. The Act of Indulgence annulling penal laws against them had been in force only three years when it was abruptly rescinded by the king, who ordered that the Act of Uniformity should again be strictly enforced. Bunyan was among the first to be tried under the new order. Convicted of having conducted religious meetings and services "in other manner than according to the Liturgie or Practice of the Church of England," he found himself back in Bedford county jail.

This time, his stay was short, lasting about six months, during which he completed the book he had started during his first imprisonment—*The Pilgrim's Progress,* a masterpiece of its kind that has kept Bunyan's name known to this day. Published in London in 1678, the book was surprisingly successful, and to no one's surprise more than Bunyan's. Two editions were sold out the first year; an enlarged version was published the next year. By the time of Bunyan's death a decade later, eight editions had appeared, and the book had been translated into French and Dutch.

In his powerfully written simple tale for simple people, Bunyan had struck a gold vein which he continued to develop. With many readers asking for a sequel, Bunyan decided to extend *Pilgrim's Progress* by adding Part II. This pictured the adventures and adversities encountered by the Pilgrim's wife Christiana and their children as they set out to follow in Christian's footsteps on his pilgrimage to the Celestial City. Published in 1684, Part II is a far inferior work, covering much of the same ground as Part I with few significant variations or additions. In these Notes, the two parts have been dealt with as separate units, each being complete in itself; one part can be read and studied with only slight reference to the other.

Bunyan had been keeping his pen going, on other things, turning out a number of religious tracts and completing three more books: *The Life and Death of Mr. Badman* (1680); *The Holy War* (1682); and *A Holy Life* (1684). He also published some moralistic verse addressed to the young: *A Book for Boys and Girls, or Country Rhimes for Children* and *Divine Emblems for Youth, or Temporal Things Spiritualized.* The verse was ragged, to say the least, but the subjects dealt with were treated interestingly in a far from solemn manner.

At the time the second part of *Pilgrim's Progress* was published, Bunyan was fifty-six, but still hale and hearty. His prison years had not sapped his health or vigor. As he had been doing for years, he zealously continued to tend the needs of brethren in his ever-growing parish and in neighboring parishes. The end came suddenly and unexpectedly as a result of a goodwill mission. One of Bunyan's young neighbors was at odds with his father. As they were seriously estranged, the young neighbor asked Bunyan for help in trying to effect a reconciliation. Able at such things and always sympathetic toward those in difficulty, Bunyan agreed and in the summer of 1688 saddled up and rode some twenty miles to the town of Reading, where the father lived.

Having paved the way for a reconciliation, Bunyan rode on to London, about forty miles away, to visit his many Baptist friends there. It was a dismal day for traveling, with a heavy rain pouring down, and he arrived in London, chilled and soaked to the skin. Along the way he had caught cold, was feverish and feeling ill. But sick as he was, Bunyan rose from bed the next Sunday and preached a sermon, as he had been expected to do, at the Baptist meetinghouse in Boar's Head Yard, off Petticoat Lane, in Whitechapel. This was Bunyan's last sermon. His illness became progressively worse; his cold developed into pneumonia, from which he died on August 31, 1688, three months short of his sixtieth birthday. His London friends buried him with simple ceremony in what was then known as Bunhill in the Fields, now Bunhill Fields, the "Camp Santo" of the Nonconformists.

Bunyan lived to see some sixty of his writings in print. With the growth of his influence as pastor and preacher, he had become known as "Bishop" Bunyan, though the Baptists had no bishops and abhorred that office and all it stood for. Bunyan always listed pride as one of the worst of sins, but he must have felt a sense of satisfaction and accomplishment as he looked back to those days when he was a semi-literate tinker's apprentice at Elstow. But the course of Bunyan's life would have been of no interest to future generations, scores of biographies would never have been written about him, if it were not for *Pilgrim's Progress*. He is not forgotten because of that single flash of genius.

ABOUT THE BOOK

As briefly noted before, *The Pilgrim's Progress*, Part I, was conceived and largely written by Bunyan while he was lying in prison, and he tells us the circumstances. He was working hard to finish another book when he conceived the idea of writing a story about the adventures that a devout Christian might meet in trying to save his soul by setting out on a pilgrimage to Heaven. Bunyan, wishing to complete the book in hand, put the new idea in the back of his mind. But it would not stay there, crowding up front and blazing through his mind "like sparks that from the coals of fire do fly." So many ideas flashed into his mind that he had a hard time in keeping notes for future use.

Bunyan scholars do not entirely agree, but generally believe that the author wrote most of *Pilgrim's Progress* (Part I) during his first long imprisonment and completed it during his second incarceration during 1675. In any case, whenever completed, Bunyan showed his manuscript to friends and asked their counsel on whether to publish it or not. Some said yes. As many said not, arguing that Bunyan had treated sacred matters in too colloquial and familiar a style and manner. Bunyan decided to go ahead, writing:

> Now was I in a strait, and did not see
> Which was the best thing to be done by me;
> At last I thought, since you are thus divided,
> I print it will, and so the case decided.

It was well for Bunyan and his fame—and his lean pocketbook—that he so decided, for what he called his "Scribble" was immediately acclaimed and enjoyed a phenomenal success. The first edition, published in London in 1678 by Nathaniel Ponder "At the Sign of the Peacock in the Poultry," was quickly sold out, requiring a second edition within the year. Next year, a third edition appeared, in which Bunyan made many revisions and added a number of scenes as afterthoughts. This third edition, the last personally revised by Bunyan, is regarded as the definitive edition of the book, and the one that has been generally published down the years. By 1688, when Bunyan died, the book had sold more than 100,000 copies, a quite fantastic figure for the time. It was soon translated into French and Dutch, and published in Puritan New England. Later, the book was translated into other languages, including even the Chinese.

The first edition had small pages, octavo in size, and ran to 332 pages. Rather messily printed on cheap paper, it sold for 1*s*.6*d*. a copy. This was within the means of those whom Bunyan wished to reach. He did not write for the literati or the carriage trade, for the nobles and others who lived in the Big Houses. He wrote for the people among whom he had been born and lived his life—humble and rather poor people, for the most part, such as he had met in the cottages of the Bedfordshire countryside. He knew and shared their way of life, their interests, their dreams. He talked their language, and they responded. That *Pilgrim's Progress*, at the time it appeared, was ridiculed and scorned by the literati, academic pundits, and polished, sophisticated aristocrats did not bother Bunyan one bit. He had found his audience, a much larger audience than any other writer of his day enjoyed.

In his writing, Bunyan commanded a good effective style. It was simple, strong, masculine, and direct, without any literary flourishes or affectations. As he more than once said, "do not affect high expressions; they will drown your children.... Words easy to be understood do often hit the mark when high and learned ones do only pierce the air." He had a very observant eye for graphic and significant detail in his descriptions of incidents, landscapes, and characters. He could tick off a character by merely giving him a name—Pliant, Obstinate, Mr. Worldly Wiseman, Evangelist, Mr. Talkative, Lord Hate-good, Mercy, Great-heart, Miss Much-afraid, et al. His syntax is often faulty, his punctuation misleading, and his spelling very erratic even by the lax standards of his day (in the seventeenth century, almost every man was his own speller). Even so, he captures and holds the reader's attention, and knows how to keep his story going except in those passages where he gets his characters involved in long conversations about abstruse points of theology.

To Bunyan, there were angels, and they were real, not merely symbolic. So, too, were fiends, devils, giants, and hideous monsters. Bunyan could describe them so well because he had seen them and encountered them in the hallucinations and nightmares to which he was subject in his younger years. Bunyan accepted dreams as real, as well as prophetic. He never forgot the time he "saw" God, "wrapped all in fire," riding a dark thunderhead in the sky and scowling down on the earth as if about to hurl a thunderbolt to destroy it in a single blinding flash.

In approaching his audience, whether in sermons or in writing, Bunyan first "preached terror," as he himself tells us, condemning all the weaknesses of the flesh and pointing out all the awful threats of "the Law." After his audience had been softened up a bit, as it were, he would offer sinners—and, in his mind, almost everybody was a sinner—the consolation and hope that they could save their souls and enjoy eternal life of unspeakable joy in Heaven if they opened their hearts to Christ's love. He would forgive all their sins if they mended their ways, and conscientiously kept at it. This methodology Bunyan followed in arranging the scenes and episodes in *Pilgrim's Progress:* first a fall or a block, then redemption.

In his theological views, Bunyan was what is now known as a Fundamentalist. He believed in the Bible from cover to cover. Everything worth knowing was spelled out in Holy Writ. All things had happened just as the Book said they had. The world was created in seven days; Adam and Eve had been evicted from the Garden of Eden for eating an apple (one of Bunyan's Pilgrims was shown such an apple from the Garden); Lot's wife had been turned into a pillar of salt (Bunyan believed it was still to be seen in the Middle East); the waters of the Red Sea had been miraculously parted for the escape of the Israelites from bondage in Egypt; Moses had struck a rock with his rod and out gushed a stream of cold, clear spring water to quench the thirst of his desperately parched followers (Bunyan's hero, Christian, was shown Moses' rod, as well as the slingshot and the very stone with which David had slain Goliath); angels hovered everywhere, with Satan always just around the corner.

Bunyan would have been simply horrified by interpretations given to Scripture by modern divines. As for philosophic studies in comparative religion, he would have regarded them as the sheerest blasphemy. There was only one religion, the Christian, as appended to the ancient Hebraic—and not all of the Christian either, only the Protestant branch—and not all of that branch either, only that of English Puritanism.

To understand Bunyan and what he is saying in *Pilgrim's Progress*, it is essential to understand the origin, background, and effects of the Puritan movement which so deeply affected England and our own country as well through the powerful influence of Puritan New England. After his break from the Roman Catholic Church in the early 1500s, less for doctrinal reasons than for reasons of state, Henry VIII set up his own church, the Church of England, with himself virtually as pope. The king was not a Protestant, and did not propose to become one, keeping most of Roman ritual and belief. His was an official church, a state church, to which everyone had to belong and pay tithes. No other form of worship was tolerated.

Under Henry's successors, an increasing number began to find fault with that church, objecting that it was corrupt and slothful (as it was in part), and that many of its practices were "unlawful," that is, there was no warrant for them in the Bible. The more these men dug into Scripture, the less justification could they find for a great deal of current belief and observance. The originally simple Christian faith, they declared, had been corrupted by time and "human invention." The imperative need was to restore it to its "ancient puritie"—or, as our American

Pilgrim Forefathers phrased it, "to its primative order, libertie, and bewtie." These views upset the orthodox, especially the ecclesiastical hierarchy. In 1565, Archbishop Parker denounced those holding such views as "these precise men." They were first dubbed the Precisians, but soon became known as the Puritans—so named, it should be observed, for their theological doctrine, not for their moral and social code, which developed later.

The Puritans sought a simple church structure, with no superstructure of bishops, archbishops, deans, and such officers. Where in the Bible could one find "warrant" for such officers? Every congregation should be more or less on its own, choosing its own minister, or pastor, or "teacher," without any dictation from outside. The congregation should be a democratic fellowship, with each communicant establishing his or her own relationship with God without benefit of clergy. The minister might help to guide them, of course, but the best guide was to read the Bible assiduously, which Bunyan had done. It was this need for each individual to establish his own unique personal relationship with God that led the Puritan to his zeal amounting at times to fanaticism, to his continuous soul-searching, to his self-righteous disposition to criticize and belittle those who did not see eye to eye with him and, above all, to his overpowering sense of guilt about his derelictions, however trivial—so great and oppressive a feeling of guilt that it once almost swamped Bunyan and is evident in all of his works.

Pilgrim's Progress is a Puritan story, and Bunyan chose to tell it in the form of an allegory, a form with which he was familiar from his reading, however sketchy that may have been except for the Bible and the *Book of Martyrs.* In addition, Bunyan chose to present his allegory in the form of a dream, which gave the widest latitude to his always fertile and often rather fevered imagination.

Bunyan's was a simple mind which did not deal in logic, reason, or abstractions. These were beyond the grasp of Bunyan, who saw the world and projected it in the form of visual images, in a sort of fantasy, and yet his dreams and visions are clear and consistently sound, having an inner logic of their own that makes them as complete and meaningful as ordinary perceptions. Bunyan had an extraordinary gift for pictorializing and personifying abstractions, and for transforming what would otherwise have been dull arguments and pedantic verbalistics into shining metaphor, into parable, into allegory, filled with movement, life, and color. Heightening the effects achieved by Bunyan, there is a rough poetic quality in his prose, though the snatches of verse he interspersed in his texts are without exception execrable.

George Bernard Shaw, in the preface to his play *Man and Superman*, declared his opinion that, as a dramatic writer, Bunyan is "better than Shakespeare." One suspects that G. B. S. is here pulling our leg, as he so liked to do, and did so well, so often. In any case, this may be said of *Pilgrim's Progress:* with its allegorical form and content, it is the best of its kind in the language and will never be matched, for no one in our scientific, atomic, skeptical age could or would attempt anything like it. At the very least, we can examine, appraise, and perhaps admire the work as an antique three centuries old, reflecting the tastes and craftsmanship of a vanished era with a very different way and view of life.

Part I

SYNOPSIS

In this section events are reviewed according to principal scenes of action. Place names appear in the order in which major incidents occur.

City of Destruction

The city stands as a symbol of the entire world as it is, with all of its sins, corruptions, and sorrows. No one living there can have any hope of salvation. Convinced that the city is about to be blasted by the wrath of God, Christian flees and sets out alone on a pilgrimage which he hopes will lead him to Mount Zion, to the Celestial City, where he can enjoy eternal life in the happy company of God and the Heavenly Host.

Slough of Despond

A swamp, a bog, a quagmire, the first obstacle in Christian's course. Pilgrims are apt to get mired down here by their doubts and fears. After much difficulty and with some providential help, Christian finally manages to flounder across the treacherous bog and is on his way again.

Village of Morality

Near the village Christian meets Mr. Worldly Wiseman, who, though not religiously inclined, is a friendly and well-disposed person. He tells Christian that it would be foolish of him to continue his pilgrimage, the end of which could only be hunger, pain, and death. Christian should be a sensible fellow and settle down in the Village of Morality. It would be a good place to raise a family, for living was cheap there and they would have honest, well-behaved people as neighbors—people who lived by the Ten Commandments.

More than a little tempted by this, Christian decides that he should at least have a look at Morality. But along the way he is stopped by his friend Evangelist, who berates him sharply for having listened to anything Mr. Worldly Wiseman might have to say. If Christian is seriously interested in saving his soul, he would be well advised to get back as quickly as possible on the path to the Wicket Gate which Evangelist had pointed out to him before.

Wicket Gate

Arriving almost out of breath, Christian reads the sign on the gate: "Knock and it shall be opened unto you." He knocks a number of times before arousing the gatekeeper, a "grave person" named Good-will, who comes out to ask what Christian wants. After the latter has explained his mission, he is let through the gate, which opens on the Holy Way, a straight and narrow path leading toward the Celestial City. Christian asks if he can now be relieved of the heavy burden—a sack filled with his sins and woes—that he has been carrying on his back for so long. Good-will replies that he cannot help him, but that if all goes well, Christian will be freed of his burden in due course.

Interpreter's House

On Good-will's advice, Christian makes his first stop at the large house of Interpreter, a character symbolizing the Holy Spirit. Interpreter shows his guest a number of "excellent things." These include a portrait of the ideal pastor with the Bible in his hand and a crown of gold on his head; a dusty parlor which is like the human heart before it is cleansed with the Gospel; a sinner in an iron cage, an apostate doomed to suffer the torments of Hell through all eternity; a wall with a fire burning against it. A figure (the Devil himself) is busily throwing water on the fire to put it out. But he would never succeed, Interpreter explains, because the fire represents the divine spirit in the human heart and a figure on the far side of the wall keeps the fire burning brightly by secretly pouring oil on it— "the oil of Christ's Grace."

The Cross

Beyond Interpreter's House, Christian comes to the Cross, which stands on higher ground beside the Holy Way. Below it, at the foot of the gentle slope, is an open sepulchre. When Christian stops by the Cross, the burden on his back suddenly slips from his shoulders, rolls down the slope, and falls into the open sepulchre, to be seen no more. As Christian stands weeping with joy, three Shining Ones (angels) appear. They tell him all his sins are now forgiven, give him bright new raiment to replace his old ragged clothes, and hand him a parchment, "a Roll with a seal upon it." For his edification and instruction, Christian is to read the Roll as he goes along, and when he reaches the Pearly Gates, he is to present it as his credentials—a sort of passport to Heaven, as it were.

Difficulty Hill

The Holy Way beyond the Cross is fenced in with a high wall on either side. The walls have been erected to force all aspiring Pilgrims to enter the Holy Way in the proper manner, through the Wicket Gate. As Christian is passing along, two men—Formalist and Hypocrisy—climb over the wall and drop down beside him. Christian finds fault with this and gives the wall-jumpers a lecture on the dangers of trying shortcuts. They have been successfully taking shortcuts all their lives, the intruders reply, and all will go well this time.

Not too pleased with his company, Christian proceeds with Hypocrisy and Formalist to the foot of Difficulty Hill, where three paths join and they must make a choice. One path goes straight ahead up the steep slope of the hill; another goes around the base of the hill to the right; the third, around the hill to the left. Christian argues that the right path is the one leading straight ahead up Difficulty Hill. Not liking the prospect of much exertion, Formalist and Hypocrisy decide to take the easier way on the level paths going around the hill. Both get lost and perish.

Halfway up Difficulty Hill, so steep in places that he has to inch forward on hands and knees, Christian comes to a pleasant arbor provided for the comfort of weary Pilgrims. Sitting down to rest, Christian reaches into his blouse and takes out his precious Roll. While reading it, he drops off to sleep, being awakened when he hears a voice saying sternly: "Go to the ant, thou sluggard; consider her ways, and be wise."

Jumping up, Christian makes with all speed to the top of the hill, where he meets two Pilgrims coming toward him—Timorous and Mistrust. They have been up ahead, they say, and there are lions there. They are giving up their pilgrimage and returning home, and unsuccessfully try to persuade Christian to come with them. Their report about the lions disturbs Christian, who reaches into his blouse to get his Roll so that he may read it and be comforted. To his consternation, the Roll is not there.

Carefully searching along the way, Christian retraces his steps to the arbor, where, as he recalls, he had been reading the Roll when he allowed himself to doze off in "sinful sleep." Not finding his treasure immediately, he sits down and weeps, considering himself utterly undone by his carelessness in losing "his pass into the Celestial City." When in deepest despair, he chances to see something lying half-covered in the grass. It is his precious Roll, which he tucks away securely in his blouse. Having offered a prayer of thanks "to God for directing his eye to the place where it lay," Christian wearily climbs back to the top of Difficulty Hill. From there he sees a stately building and as it is getting on toward dark, hastens there.

Palace Beautiful

A narrow path leads off the Holy Way to the lodge in front of Palace Beautiful. Starting up the path, Christian sees two lions, stops, and turns around as if to retreat. The porter at the lodge, Watchful, who has been observing him, calls out that there is nothing to be afraid of if one has faith. The lions are chained, one on either side of the path, and anyone with faith can pass safely between them if he keeps carefully to the middle of the path, which Christian does.

Arriving at the lodge, he asks if he can get lodging for the night. The porter, Watchful, replies that he will find out from those in charge of Palace Beautiful. Soon, four virgins come out to the lodge, all of them "grave and beautiful damsels": Discretion, Prudence, Piety, and Charity. Satisfied with Christian's answers to their questions, they invite him in, introduce him to the rest of the family, serve him supper, and assign him to a beautiful bedroom – Peace – for the night.

Next morning, the virgins show him the "rarities" of the place: first, the library, filled with ancient documents dating back to the beginning of time; next, the armory, packed with swords, shields, helmets, breastplates, and other things sufficient to equip all servants of the Lord, even if they were as numerous as the stars in the sky. Leading their guest to the roof of the palace, the virgins point to mountains in the distance – the Delectable Mountains, which lie on the way to the Celestial City. Before allowing Christian to depart, the virgins give him arms and armor to protect himself during the next stretch of his journey, which they warn will be dangerous.

Valley of Humiliation

Here Christian is attacked and almost overcome by a "foul fiend" named Apollyon – a hideous monster with scales like a fish, wings like a dragon, mouth like a lion, and feet like a bear; flames and smoke belch out of a hole in his belly. Christian, after a painful struggle, wounds the fiend with his sword and drives him off.

Valley of the Shadow of Death

This is a wilderness, a land of deserts and pits, inhabited only by yowling hobgoblins and other dreadful creatures. The path here is very narrow, edged on one side by a deep, water-filled ditch in which many have drowned; on the other side, by a treacherous bog. Walking carefully, Christian goes on and soon finds himself close to the open mouth of Hell, the Burning Pit, out of which comes a cloud of noxious fumes, long fingers of fire, showers of sparks, and hideous noises. With flames flickering all around and smoke almost choking him, Christian manages to get through by use of "All-prayer."

Nearing the end of the valley, he hears a shout raised by someone up ahead: "Though I walk through the Valley of the Shadow of Death, I will fear none ill, for Thou art with me." As only a Pilgrim could have raised that cry, Christian hastens forward to see who it might be. To his surprise and delight he finds that it is an old friend, Faithful, one of his neighbors in the City of Destruction.

Vanity Fair

Happily journeying together, exchanging stories about their adventures and misadventures, the two Pilgrims come to the town of Vanity Fair, through which they must pass. Interested only in commerce and money-making, the town holds a year-round fair at which all kinds of things are bought and sold—"houses, lands, trades, titles, . . . lusts, pleasures, . . . bodies, souls, silver, gold, pearls, precious stones, and what not." Christian and Faithful infuriate the merchandisers by turning up their noses at the wares offered them, saying that they would buy nothing but the Truth. Their presence and their attitude cause a hubbub in the town, which leads the authorities to jail them for disturbing the peace. The prisoners conduct themselves so well that they win the sympathy of many townspeople, producing more strife and commotion in the streets, and the prisoners are held responsible for this, too, though they have done nothing.

It is decided to indict them on the charge of disrupting trade, creating dissension, and treating with contempt the customs and laws laid down for the town by its prince, old Beelzebub himself. Brought to trial first, Faithful is convicted and sentenced to be executed in the manner prescribed by the presiding judge, Lord Hate-good. The hapless Faithful is scourged, brutally beaten, lanced with knives, stoned, and then burned to ashes at the stake. Thus, he becomes another of the Christian martyrs assured of enjoying eternal bliss up on high.

Doubting Castle and Giant Despair

In a manner only vaguely explained, Christian gets free and goes on his way—but not alone, for he has been joined by Hopeful, a native of Vanity Fair who is fleeing in search of better things. After a few minor adventures, the two reach a sparkling stream, the River of the Water of Life, which meanders through beautiful meadows bright with flowers. For a time the Holy Way follows the river bank but then veers off into rougher ground which is hard on the sore tired feet of the travelers. Wishing there were an easier way, they plod along until they come to another meadow behind a high fence. Having climbed the fence to have a look, Christian persuades Hopeful that they should move over into By-path Meadow, where there is a soft grassy path paralleling theirs.

Moving along, they catch up with Vain-confidence, who says that he is bound for the Celestial City and knows the way perfectly. Night comes on, but he continues to push ahead briskly, with Christian and Hopeful following. Suddenly, the latter hear a frightened cry and a loud thud. Vain-confidence has been dashed to pieces by falling into a deep pit dug by the owner of the meadow. Christian and Hopeful retreat, but as they can see nothing in the dark, they decide to lie down in the meadow to pass the night.

Next morning, they are surprised and seized by the prince of By-path Meadow, a giant named Despair. Charging them with malicious trespassing, he hauls them to his stronghold, Doubting Castle, and throws them into a deep dark dungeon, where they lie for days without food or drink. At length, Giant Despair appears, beats them almost senseless, and advises them to take their own lives so that he will not have to come back to finish them off himself. When all seems hopeless, Christian suddenly brightens up, "as one half amazed," and exclaims: "What a fool am I, thus to lie in a stinking dungeon when I may as well walk at liberty. I have a key in my bosom called Promise which will (I am persuaded) open any lock in Doubting Castle."

Finding that the magic key works, the prisoners are soon out in the open and running as fast as they can to get back onto the Holy Way, where they erect a sign warning other Pilgrims against being tempted by the apparent ease of traveling by way of By-path Meadow.

Delectable Mountains

Christian and Hopeful next come to the Delectable Mountains, where they find gardens, orchards, vineyards, and fountains of water. Four shepherds—Experience, Knowledge, Watchful, and Sincere—come to greet them, telling them that the mountains are the Lord's, as are the flocks of sheep grazing there. Having been escorted around the mountains and shown the sights there, the two Pilgrims on the eve of their departure receive from the shepherds a paper instructing them on what to do and what to avoid on the journey ahead. For one thing, they should not lie down and sleep in the Enchanted Ground, for that would be fatal.

Country of Beulah

This is a happy land where the sun shines day and night, flowers bloom continuously, and the sweet and pleasant air is filled with birdsong. There is no lack of grain and wine. Christian and Hopeful stop to rest and enjoy themselves here, pleased that the Celestial City is now within sight, which leads them to assume that the way there is now clear.

Dark River

Proceeding, they are amazed when they come to the Dark River, a wide, swift-flowing stream. They look around for a bridge or boat on which to cross. A Shining One appears and tells them that they must make their way across as best they can, that fording the river is a test of faith, that those with faith have nothing to fear. Wading into the river, Hopeful finds firm footing, but Christian does not. He is soon floundering in water over his head, fearing that he will be drowned, that he will never see "the land that flows with milk and honey." Hopeful helps Christian by holding his head above water, and the two finally achieve the crossing.

Celestial City

On the far side of the river, two Shining Ones are waiting for the Pilgrims and take them by the arm to assist them in climbing the steep slope to the Celestial City, which stands on a "mighty hill. . . . higher than the clouds." Coming to the gate of the city, built all of precious stones, Christian and Hopeful present their credentials, which are taken to the King (God). He orders the gate to be opened, and the two weary but elated Pilgrims go in, to find that the streets are paved with gold and that along them walk many men with crowns on their heads and golden harps in their hands.

LIST OF CHARACTERS

Part I of the book has only one main character, Christian, the Pilgrim. He appears in every scene and dominates them all. Other characters are those he chances to meet on his journey and with whom he talks for a longer or shorter time. Only two of them, Faithful and Hopeful, share any of his experiences.

Christian

A poor, ragged man who flees from the wicked City of Destruction, convinced that God is about to blast it for its sins, and sets out on a pilgrimage to find the Celestial City, where his soul will be saved and he can live for all eternity in the company of God, and of the Heavenly Host.

Evangelist

Preacher of the Holy Word, always eager to help those who are seriously concerned about the state of their souls and about finding the way to Heaven.

Obstinate

Who accepts things as they are, resisting any change, and thinks anyone undertaking a pilgrimage like Christian's is a fool, out of his mind.

Pliant

A well-intentioned man who decides to join Christian on his pilgrimage but, having little courage and less resolution, turns back at the first obstacle.

Mr. Worldly Wiseman

Knows the world and has come to terms with it on a high moral level. A generous and sympathetic man, he obeys the Ten Commandments and lives in great esteem among his friends and neighbors. With his plausibility he almost seduces Christian in advising him to settle down in the village of Morality instead of going on toward the Celestial City.

Good-will

Keeper of the Wicket Gate, entrance to the Holy Way, or "King's Highway," leading to the Celestial City on Mount Zion.

Interpreter

The Holy Spirit which inhabits a large house that Christian visits and where he is shown many wonders and given a number of exhortations on the way he should go.

Three Shining Ones

Angels who meet Christian at the Cross.

Formalist and Hypocrisy

Formalist is one of those who knows all the outward forms of religion, but not the inner spirit. The Gospel is in his head, not in his heart. Hypocrisy is what his name implies, being all things to all men. Both Formalist and Hypocrisy come to a bad end at the foot of Difficulty Hill.

Discretion, Prudence, Piety, and Charity

Virgins in charge of Palace Beautiful, where Christian rests for several days and is shown the "rarities" of the place.

Apollyon

A foul fiend whom Christian encounters in the Valley of Humiliation. The monster has scales like a fish, wings like a dragon, feet like a bear, and a mouth like a lion. Out of a hole in his belly belch smoke and flame. Christian has a narrow escape from death when Apollyon attacks him.

Faithful

A townsman from the City of Destruction whom Christian meets as he emerges from the Valley of the Shadow of Death. The two Pilgrims go along together until Faithful meets his death by execution at Vanity Fair.

Mr. Talkative

One of those willing to discuss anything, often very sensibly, but never willing to do anything. "Good riddance," says Christian when Talkative decides to go his own way to salvation.

Lord Hate-good

The judge who sentences Faithful to a frightful death at Vanity Fair.

Hopeful

A refugee from Vanity Fair who joins Christian, and the two of them go on together all the way to the Celestial City.

By-ends

From the wealthy town of Fair-speech, By-ends likes religion when it "goes in silver slippers," with the sun shining and the people applauding. By-ends is a nickname given to him by friends because of his knack in snatching every opportunity for profit that falls in his way.

Giant Despair

Who surprises Christian and Hopeful while asleep in By-path Meadow, seizes them as trespassers, and throws them into the cellar dungeon in his stronghold, Doubting Castle. The prisoners are about to be killed by the giant when Christian suddenly remembers that he has a magic key that will open all the doors and gates of the castle, and they escape back to the Holy Way.

Knowledge, Experience, Watchful, and Sincere

Shepherds tending the flocks of the Lord on the heights of the Delectable Mountains. The shepherds are very helpful to the Pilgrims, giving them exact directions to the Celestial City and telling them what to avoid along the way.

Ignorance

A "very brisk" lad who comes down a little crooked lane from the Country of Conceit and encounters Christian and Hopeful in the Holy Way. They think he is all wrong in his ideas, but he tells them to mind their own business. Trailing along behind, Ignorance makes it all the way to the gates of the Celestial City. But as he does not have the proper credentials, the "King" (God) has him thrown down a side pit into Hell.

Turn-away

An apostate who has been seized by seven devils, tied with seven stout cords, and is being carried off to be tossed down the side mouth to Hell which Christian and Hopeful had been shown, to their great fright, in the Delectable Mountains.

Flatterer

A "man black of flesh, but covered with a very light robe," who induces the two Pilgrims to follow him, leading them a circular course into a net from which there appears to be no means of escape. But a Shining One appears with a whipcord, cuts the net, and leads them back to the Holy Way.

Atheist

Who laughs at the Pilgrims, telling them that he has made great search and there is no such place as the Celestial City, which greatly shocks Christian and Hopeful: "What! no Mount Zion!"

SUMMARIES AND COMMENTARIES

Pilgrim's Progress was written in two parts. Each part is a long continuous narrative, without divisions. Consequently, the narrative will be dealt with in sections based on major scenes and incidents.

SECTION 1

To the Wicket Gate

Summary

Bunyan begins *Pilgrim's Progress* this way: "As I walked through the wilderness of this world, I lighted on a certain place where was a den [jail], and I laid me down in that place to sleep; and as I slept I dreamed a dream."

In his dream the author sees a poor, ragged man standing off by himself in the fields, a heavy burden on his back, a Bible in his hand. As he opens the Book to read from time to time, he weeps and trembles and cries out: "What shall I do? What shall I do to be saved?" He is convinced that the City of Destruction where he lives is about to be "burned with fire from Heaven" for its manifold sins and corruptions.

He tells his family and friends of this, and of the need to flee immediately. But they put down his distress to some "frenzy distemper [that] had got into his head." They put him to bed in the hope "that sleep might settle his brains," but that does no good. As the ragged man goes on talking about the immediate need of finding some way of escape from the doomed city, those around him begin to grow hardened about all his apocalyptic notions. In the hope of driving away his "distemper by harsh and surly carriages toward him," they chide him, deride him, and quite neglect him. He pities them and prays for them, but to no effect.

The poor, ragged, distraught man is soon given a name; appropriately, it is Christian. One day when he is walking along, reading the Bible, and crying out in spiritual torment, he is met by Evangelist, who asks Christian what is the matter, what is troubling him. Christian explains that he wishes to flee the City of Destruction to live forever in the Celestial City, but how is he going to do that, not knowing the way. Pointing across a very broad field, Evangelist asks: "Do you see yonder Wicket-gate?" (Matt. 7:13). No, says Christian. "Do you see yonder shining Light?" (Ps. 119:105; 2 Pet. 1:19). Christian thinks he does. Very well, Evangelist concludes, he should follow the Light to the Wicket Gate, where he should knock and he would there be told what to do.

At this, Christian begins to run. As he is near his house, he is seen by his wife and children, who run after him, calling out to him to return and not leave them destitute. Christian does not look back, puts his fingers in his ears to keep from hearing the pitiful wails of his family, and runs on crying: "Life! Life! Eternal Life!"

To fetch Christian back, by force if necessary, neighbors send out two men, Obstinate and Pliant. They cannot persuade Christian to return. Obstinate gives up the attempt and goes back, dismissing Christian as a "brain-sick fellow." But Pliant becomes interested in what Christian has to say and decides to join him in his pilgrimage, particularly after Christian has unfolded his vision of the wonders they will enjoy at the end of their pilgrimage. "There is an endless kingdom to be inhabited, and everlasting Life to be given us. There are crowns of glory to be given us, and garments that will make us shine like the sun in the firmament.... There shall be no more crying, nor sorrow.... There we shall be with Seraphims and Cherubims, creatures that will dazzle your eyes to look at them."

As they walk along together, Christian and Pliant are so busy talking about immortality and other things that they do not notice where they are going and suddenly fall into a bog, the Slough of Despond, where they wallow for a time. Weighted down by the burden on his back, Christian begins to sink in the mire. Pliant calls out:

"Ah, neighbor Christian, where are you now?"

"Truly. I do not know."

"Is this the happiness you have told me all this while of?" asks Pliant angrily. "If we have such ill speed at our first setting out, what may we expect 'twixt this and our journey's end."

After a struggle, Pliant pulls himself out of the swamp and, all covered with slime and mud, returns home, where his neighbors laugh at him as a fool for having become involved in such a silly venture. Christian, determined to go on, finally manages to flounder across the Slough of Despond, having received unexpected assistance from a man named Help, who suddenly appears and almost as suddenly disappears.

Proceeding, Christian soon meets with a "gentleman" named Mr. Worldly Wiseman, who offers some advice. Instead of traveling in such a burdened manner, with so many sighs and groans, Christian should give up his pilgrimage, which would certainly end only in pain, hunger, perils, "nakedness, swords, lions, dragons, darkness and, in a word, death." Rather, he should be a sensible fellow and go to the neighboring village of Morality, which Mr. Wiseman points out to him, saying that the people there are honest, law-abiding, and God-fearing; a good house can be had at a low rent; provisions of all kinds are plentiful and cheap. Besides, there is in the village a "very judicious man," Mr. Legality, who has relieved many a man of his burdens and thus cured a great number of those "crazed in their wits with their burdens."

If Christian were to send for his wife and children, the family could settle down in the village and live happily "with honest neighbors, in credit and good fashion." Christian is tempted, at least to the point of deciding to have a closer look at the village and perhaps have a talk with Mr. Legality. The way to the village leads by a steep high hill which overhangs the wayside. Christian stops, fearing that the overhang might fall on his head.

While he is standing there, not knowing what to do, he sees a figure coming toward him. It is Evangelist, and Christian begins "to blush for shame." With a "severe and dreadful countenance," Evangelist upbraids Christian for listening to Mr. Worldly Wiseman and swerving from the Holy Way. The village of Morality is a good enough place, but it is not the Celestial City. If Christian is seriously interested in saving his soul, he had better make all speed to get on the path leading to the Wicket Gate pointed out to him before by Evangelist. After a lengthy religious discourse on the "very great sin" Christian has committed, Evangelist assures him: "All manner of sin and blasphemies shall be forgiven unto men. Be not faithless, but believing" (Matt. 12:31; Mark 3:28).

Worried about whether he will be admitted, Christian starts running toward the Wicket Gate. He talks to no one along the way, going "like one that was all the while treading on forbidden ground, and could by no means think himself safe till again he was got into the way which he left to follow Mr. Worldly Wiseman's counsel."

Commentary

After the brief introduction telling the reader that what is about to be related was seen in a dream, Bunyan plunges directly into his story. Things begin happening immediately, without any of the literary preparations so often used by authors in approaching their subject. With a few swift strokes, Bunyan sharply etches the opening scene: the poor, ragged man standing off by himself, reading his Bible, and crying out with spiritual anguish; the taunts he receives as being one seized by some frenzied distemper. In describing the poor man's miseries, Bunyan had only to recall what he had written in *Grace Abounding* about the torments and taunts he had once suffered. The figure Evangelist also came out of his experience. He represents "good Mr. Gifford," the Baptist minister at Bedford, who took young Bunyan in hand and showed him the way out of his doubts and maddening anxieties.

The fact that the Pilgrim, in running away, abandons his wife and children, stopping up his ears so that he will not hear their pleas to come back, is an important point, and Bunyan comes back to it again and again. A man seeking salvation must be prepared to abandon everything in his quest for eternal bliss. He should allow no bond of affection or interest to hold him. In writing this passage, Bunyan must have had thoughts about an incident in his life that forced him to make a painful choice. Before he was first jailed for "unlawful" preaching, several sympathetic judges offered him an accommodation. He would not be prosecuted on the charges against him if he would promise to stop preaching, go home, and stay quiet. Bunyan would not promise, saying he could not do that "in good conscience," with the result that he was imprisoned for twelve years, leaving his wife and four children to live largely on charity.

As Bunyan saw it, the Slough of Despond is a rather complicated symbol. When Christian is pulled out of the swamp by Help, evidently a heavenly angel, he asks why the path from the City of Destruction to the Wicket Gate should lead through such a miry trap. Help explains that the King (God) does not like it, but has been unable to do anything about it. Numberless times he has ordered his "laborers" to build a causeway across it. Countless cart-loads of dirt have been hauled there and dumped, only to sink out of sight in the mud.

The Slough cannot be mended, Help explains, for here collects all the "scum and filth" of sin that is continually flowing, all the doubts, fears, and "discouraging apprehensions" of penitents seeking the Wicket Gate. Help adds that there are good substantial steps leading across the Slough, placed there by the lawgiver. But men usually do not see these steps or, if they do, "through the dizziness of their heads" they trip or slip off the steppingstones and plunge into the muck. The Slough of Despond is a trial that Pilgrims will always have to face as a test of faith, courage, and will.

The episode involving Mr. Worldly Wiseman and the village of Morality did not appear in the first edition of the book. Bunyan inserted it in the second to make a point that he had omitted. Mr. Worldly Wiseman, "of the town of Carnal Policy, a very great town," represents those who have made terms with the world in a good way. There is nothing mean or self-seeking about Mr. Wiseman. He is generous and always ready to help others get rid of their burdens, as he is in advising Christian to go to the village of Morality and there consult with Mr. Legality. The people in Morality are pleasant folk, God-fearing, and law-abiding, and lead a quiet, comfortable life.

Christian commits "a very great sin" in turning toward the village and away from the path chalked out for him by Evangelist, who now appears to upbraid Christian severely. The village of Morality is good enough in its way, but it is not the Celestial City. In spite of his constant church attendance and other pious observances, Mr. Worldly Wiseman is not a real Christian because he follows "only the doctrine of this world," and does not look at the world beyond. Mr. Legality is a cheat, a hypocrite, without power to relieve Christian of his burden of sin. Only God can do that. The people in the comfortable village of Morality are doomed to destruction because they are too self-satisfied and do not wrestle with their souls to assure their salvation and eternal life in the Celestial City. A conventionally religious life does not lead to those heavenly heights.

SECTION 2

Through the Wicket Gate to Interpreter's House

Summary

Reaching the little Wicket Gate, Christian sees a sign over it: "Knock and it shall be opened unto you" (Matt. 7:7). He knocks, and then again, and many more times before he arouses the gatekeeper, a "grave person" named Good-will, who comes out to ask what he wants. When Christian tells him that he was directed to the gate by Evangelist and that he is a poor burdened sinner bound for Mount Zion, Good-will unlocks the gate and gives Christian a strong pull to get him inside quickly. Why the pull? asks Christian. Because there is a strong castle near by from which Beelzebub and his minions shoot arrows at those knocking at the gate, hoping to kill them before they enter.

Under Good-will's questioning, Christian relates his adventures at length. Good-will then walks a little way with Christian to show him the way he must go, pointing out that it is a very narrow path that runs as straight as a rule can make it. Are there no turnings or windings to confuse a stranger? Yes, but Christian need not be confused if he remembers there is only one right path, "That only being straight and narrow" (Matt. 7:14).

Good-will directs Christian to the house of Interpreter, saying the latter would show him "excellent things." Arriving there, Christian knocks and knocks before a man comes to the door. Christian asks to speak with the master of the house, who in time appears and invites the traveler to come in to see things that will help him in his journey. Commanding his man to light "the candle," Interpreter leads Christian into a private room, where there is a picture of a "very grave person" hanging on the wall. "It had eyes lifted up to Heaven, the best of Books in his hand, the Law of Truth was written upon his lips, the world was behind his back. It stood as if it pleaded with men, and a crown of gold did hang over his head." The picture, explains Interpreter, is that of one of many sincere, inspiring preachers of the Gospel, a man of God, and Christian should mark his features well and remember them so that he will be able to distinguish any pious pretenders who may try to mislead him on his journey.

Leading Christian into a very large parlor full of dust, Interpreter calls for a man to sweep out the room. The latter raises such a cloud of dust that Christian all but chokes. Turning to a damsel standing by, Interpreter asks her, "Bring hither water and sprinkle the room." As soon as that is done, the room is "swept and cleansed with pleasure." When Christian asks the meaning of this, Interpreter tells him that the parlor is the heart of man, which has to be swept out to remove the dust of "Original Sin and inward corruptions," and that the damsel with her water is the Gospel that makes the soul clean and "consequently fit for the King of Glory to inhabit" (John 15:3; Eph. 5:26; Acts 15:9; Rom. 16:25, 26).

After a visit to two small children—Passion (the bad boy, wanting everything here and now) and Patience (the good boy, willing to wait for his reward in Heaven)—Interpreter takes Christian to a place where there is a fire burning against a wall. By the fire is a sinister figure constantly throwing water on the blaze to put it out. But the fire gets higher and hotter because a man on the other side of the wall is secretly adding fuel to the flames from a vessel of oil—"the oil of Christ's Grace." Do what he may, the Devil will never extinguish the flame kindled in the hearts of men as a work of Grace.

Christian is next led to a place where stands a stately beautiful palace. In front of it is gathered a large crowd anxious to get in. But in the doorway stands a troop of armed men to keep everybody out. It is not that the people in the palace want to keep people out. It is that Satan has posted the soldiers to intimidate the crowd and prevent anyone from entering.

Off to the side sits a man with a pen and inkhorn on the table before him, ready to register in a book the names of those deemed worthy to enter the palace. A man of "very stout countenance" approaches and says: "Set down my name, sir." That done, the man draws his sword, puts on his helmet, and rushes upon the soldiers in the doorway, who wound him many times. But the man, "cutting and hacking most fiercely," finally presses through the soldiers and into the palace, and those outside hear a pleasant voice welcoming him:

> Come in, come in;
> Eternal glory thou shalt win.

Christian suggests that he had better be on his way now, but Interpreter has some other things to show him, leading him into a very dark room where there is a man in an iron cage. Christian talks with the dejected man in the iron cage of Despair and learns that the prisoner was once a "fair and flourishing" Christian, with good hopes of getting to the Celestial City. But tempted by the lusts, pleasures, and profits of this world, he had fallen by the wayside, renounced the Faith, and become an apostate—a sin against the Holy Ghost for which he can never be forgiven. Through all eternity he must suffer the tortures of Hell.

Christian again suggests that he should be going, but Interpreter insists on showing him one more thing, leading him into a chamber where a man is getting up from bed and violently trembling as he dresses himself. He is shaking because of a dream he just had, and he proceeds to relate it. In the dream, the skies suddenly grew very black, with great lightning and thunder. A trumpet sounds as a man sitting on a cloud appears with his heavenly attendants around him, "all in flaming fire," and a voice rings out: "Arise ye dead, and come to Judgment!"

Rocks split asunder, graves open up, the dead emerge. Some are "exceeding happy" and hopefully look upward. Others try "to hide themselves under the mountains" (Isa. 26:21; Mic. 7:16, 17; Ps. 50:1-3). The man on the cloud orders his attendants to go among the resurrected to "gather together the tares, the chaff, and stubble, and cast them into the burning lake." To receive the chaff, the bottomless pit opens up and out of it comes hellish smoke and flames, "with hideous noises." At another order, "Gather my wheat into my garner," angels come winging down, catch up many, and carry them away into the clouds.

When Christian asks what was so frightening about that, the dreamer replies that he thought the Day of Judgment had come, and he was not ready for it. His conscience greatly troubled him. Besides, he could see that the "Judge" (the man on the cloud) was closely watching him, "showing indignation in his countenance."

Now content to let the Pilgrim be on his way, Interpreter first questions him on whether he has understood the deeper meaning of all the "excellent things" he has been shown, and whether he will always remember the lessons they have taught. Assuring Interpreter that he will never forget, Christian girds up his loins and is off, still burdened by the sack of sins on his back.

Commentary

The pace of the narrative slows up in this section, with Christian largely occupied in sightseeing and listening to Interpreter's lengthy discourse, filled with biblical quotations and allusions, as he expounds the deeper meaning of the sights. Only one thing he does not explain, and there is no need, for Christian catches the point immediately. It is the scene in which the man of "stout countenance" registers as a Christian, draws his sword, and forces his way through soldiers blocking his way into one of the Lord's castles. "I think verily I know the meaning of this," Christian remarks. A true Pilgrim has to be in fact, as well as in name, a Christian soldier, armed to defend himself and ready to whack his way through any who try to block his way to salvation.

SECTION 3

The Cross and Difficulty Hill

Summary

Proceeding from Interpreter's House, Christian comes to higher ground on which stands a Cross. Below it, down the slope, is an open sepulchre. Just as Christian reaches the Cross, the heavy bundle on his back slips from his shoulders, rolls down the slope, and falls into the sepulchre, to be seen no more. As Christian stands weeping with joy, three "Shining Ones" (angels) appear. One tells him that all of his sins are now forgiven. Another strips him of his rags, and clothes him in bright new raiment. The third puts a mark on his forehead and hands him a parchment, "a Roll with a seal upon it." This Roll he should read as he journeys along and when he gets to the Celestial Gate, he should present it as his credentials, as his passport to Heaven so to speak.

Giving three leaps for joy, Christian goes along singing until he comes upon three men lying asleep on the ground—Simple, Sloth, and Presumption. He feels duty-bound to wake them up and warn them of the great danger they are in if they do not get up and be on their way.

A lion might come by and eat them up. Saying that they can see no danger, the three turn over and go to sleep again, which leaves Christian "troubled to think that men in that danger should so little esteem the kindness of him that so freely offered to help them."

Still musing about such ingratitude, Christian is proceeding along the Holy Way when he sees two men come tumbling over one of the high walls that line the narrow way. The walls had been built to prevent any from entering the Holy Way except through the Wicket Gate. The wall-jumpers – Formalist and Hypocrisy – identify themselves by saying that they come from "the land of Vain-glory and are going for praise to Mount Zion." But why had they not come in by the Wicket Gate, which was the proper way? asks Christian. Surely they must know "that he that cometh not in by the door, but climbeth up some other way, the same is a thief and a robber" (John 10:1).

It was too far around to the Wicket Gate, they reply, so they had followed their usual course in taking a shortcut. When Christian raises a doubt about their reception at the Celestial Gate, they tell him not to bother his head about that; their reception would be as good as his. Not very pleased with his company, Christian proceeds with Hypocrisy and Formalist to the foot of Difficulty Hill, where there are three paths and they must make a choice. One path goes straight ahead, right up the steep face of the hill; another goes around the base to the left; the third around the other way. Recalling Good-will's instructions, Christian knows that the right path is that going straight ahead up the hill. Not liking that prospect, Formalist and Hypocrisy decide to take the level paths going around the hill. Both get lost and perish.

Clambering up the hill, in places so steep that he has to crawl on hands and knees, Christian comes to a pleasant arbor, "made by the Lord of the hill for the refreshing of weary travelers." Sitting down to rest, he takes out his Roll to read, which comforts him. But reading makes him drowsy, and he falls into a fast sleep, from which he is awakened after a time by someone saying: "Go to the ant, thou sluggard; consider her ways, and be wise" (Prov. 6:6).

Jumping up, Christian speeds as fast as he can to the top of the hill, where he meets two returning Pilgrims, Timorous and Mistrust. What's the matter that you run the wrong way? asks Christian. Because there are lions ahead, they reply, adding that "the further we go, the more danger we meet with," so they were turning back and returning home.

They advise Christian to come with them, but the latter decides to venture on. There might be death ahead, but death was certain if he went back to the City of Destruction, which was being "prepared for fire and brimstone." Still, the reports of Timorous and Mistrust were disturbing. To find solace and encouragement in reading it, Christian reaches into his blouse for his Roll, but it is not there.

Shocked, moaning and groaning, loudly bewailing his carelessness in having lost his "pass into the Celestial City," Christian recalls that he had last had his Roll in the arbor and retraces his steps there. Not finding his treasure immediately, he is in utter despair and sits weeping when, suddenly, he spies the Roll, which had fallen from his lap during his "sinful sleep." Offering "thanks to God for directing his eye to the place where it lay," Christian tucks the Roll securely in his blouse and painfully climbs back to the top of the hill. From there he sees a stately palace not too far away. As it is getting on toward dark he hastens there.

Commentary

The symbolism of the Cross and the open sepulchre, and of Christian's release from the heavy burden of sin he has been carrying, is obvious, as is the appearance of the three Shining Ones who give him new raiment and the Roll that identifies him as one of the chosen, one of the Elect. Christian is very proud of the embroidered white coat he has been given. It is not only beautiful in itself, but is another tangible token of God's favor. When he meets them, Hypocrisy and Formalist scoff at this, saying that the coat was given to him by neighbors to hide the shame of his nakedness, and laugh when Christian tells them that the Roll in his hand will open the gates of Heaven to him.

The significance of Difficulty Hill is also plain. Though it runs straight, the path to Heaven has its ups and downs, and the ups must be surmounted. They cannot safely be avoided. There is no easy way around them, as Formalist and Hypocrisy learn to their cost. Nothing much happens on Difficulty Hill. It stands there, it almost seems, merely to be climbed as a test of faith and endurance. Attaining the summit offers no new revelation.

Christian's only difficulty comes halfway up the hill when he falls asleep in the pleasant arbor there and loses his precious Roll. Going on, he discovers his loss and has to retrace his steps to the arbor. To point a lesson, Bunyan has Christian reproach himself severely and at length "for being so foolish as to fall asleep in that place." He now sees that

God had provided the arbor not for "sinful sleep" but only for "a little refreshing" for weary travelers along the Holy Way.

"O wretched man that I am, that I should sleep in the daytime! [Rev. 2:5; 1 Thess. 5:7-8] That I should sleep in the midst of difficulty! That I should so indulge the flesh as to use that rest for ease of my flesh which the Lord of the hill had erected only for the relief of the spirits of Pilgrims! How many steps have I took in vain!" God forgives him and directs his eye to where the missing Roll is lying. Gathering it up, Christian toils laboriously back to the top of the hill, still having the "evil of sleeping" in mind.

SECTION 4

Palace Beautiful

Summary

The palace stands a little off the Holy Way, being approached by a narrow lane leading to a lodge, or gatehouse. Starting up the lane, Christian has not gone far when he sees two lions in front of him. He stops and turns as if to go back. The porter at the lodge has been observing him and calls out: "Is thy strength so small? Fear not the lions, for they are chained, and are placed there for trial of faith where it is, and for discovery of those that have none. Keep in the midst of the path, and no hurt shall come to thee."

Taking heart, but still trembling, Christian advances warily, taking good care to walk exactly in the middle of the path as directed. Straining at their chains, the lions roar at him but cannot reach him. Clapping his hands at having safely passed between them, Christian arrives at the lodge, where he asks Watchful, the porter, "What house is this?" He is told that it was built by the Lord of the hill for the relief and security of Pilgrims. He then asks if he might spend the night. Watchful says that he will find out by summoning one of the virgins in charge of the establishment. "A grave and beautiful damsel" named Discretion appears, soon followed by three other virgins—Prudence, Piety, and Charity. Satisfied with Christian's answers to their queries, they invite him to come into Palace Beautiful, introduce him to the rest of the family, give him drink, and sit him down to supper at a table "furnished with fat things and with wine well refined."

In a lengthy conversation the virgins question Christian about himself: why did he set out on his pilgrimage; what has he seen and encountered on his journey? (Bunyan once again, for the third time, tells the reader what he has already been told about Christian's adventures and misadventures.) Has he a family? Charity inquires. When Christian replies that he has a wife and four children, Charity then asks why he had not brought them with him. Because they would not come, says Christian, and he begins to weep. He had tried time and again to persuade them, but to no avail. His wife was afraid to give up this world on the chance of finding a better one. As for his children, they were "given to the foolish delights of youth; so what by one thing, and what by another, they left me to wander in this manner alone."

Next day, the virgins show their guest the "rarities" of the place, first taking him to the study, which is filled with ancient documents dating back to the beginning of time. One is a unique document (never seen before or since), "the pedigree of the Lord of the hill, that he was the son of the Ancient of Days and came by an eternal generation." They read aloud about "some of the worthy acts that some of his servants had done: as how they had subdued kingdoms, wrought righteousness, obtained promises, stopped the mouths of lions, quenched the violence of fire, escaped the edge of the sword; out of weakness were made strong, waxed valiant in fight, and turned to flight the armies of the aliens."

Christian is then taken to the armory and shown things the Lord provides for Pilgrims, such as "sword, shield, helmet, breastplate, All-prayer, and shoes that would not wear out," and all these items in quantity sufficient to equip "as many men for the service of the Lord as there be stars in the Heaven." The armory is something of a historical museum, too, and Christian is shown some really remarkable things that deeply impress him: Moses' rod, the jawbone with which Samson wrought such havoc among the Philistines, the slingshot and the very stone with which David slew Goliath of Gath, and the sword "with which the Lord will kill the man of sin in the day that he shall rise up to the prey."

Escorting Christian to the palace roof, the virgins point to mountains in the distance. Those are the Delectable Mountains, they tell him, and his path will take him there, where he will find great comfort among the shepherds of the Lord. But the path is difficult, and the next stretch is particularly dangerous, they warn him and, as he is leaving, take him to the armory again and give him a sword, a helmet, a shield, and a breastplate for his protection along the way.

Commentary

Palace Beautiful, the virgins, and the family living here represent the church and church-fellowship, and emphasize the important role that women played in founding and sustaining the Bedford nonconformist congregation which Bunyan joined when his religious doubts were resolved. In his day the church was not only the religious center, but also the social center in the village, the place where the faithful met regularly to renew bonds of fellowship. The church was a refreshing oasis in a world of care and woe in which man too often felt isolated and alone in facing his troubles. He needed not only divine guidance but the human warmth to be found in close association with his fellows in pursuit of a common goal.

Enjoying the company and "heavenly discourse" at Palace Beautiful, Christian stays several days, longer than at any other stop on his pilgrimage. He sleeps comfortably and contentedly in a large upper chamber named Peace, which has a wide window opening toward the sunrise. In the morning Christian is up at daybreak, singing joyously:

> Where am I now? Is this the love and care
> Of Jesus for the men that Pilgrims are
> Thus to provide! That I should be forgiven!
> And dwell already the next door to Heaven!

Bunyan is never at his best when he turns to verse; his is always rough and ragged.

The two lions along the path leading to Palace Beautiful were used by Bunyan to represent the civil and ecclesiastical authorities who had been enjoined by law to suppress all nonconformist congregations. Bunyan himself had run foul of that law and been jailed for twelve years for his beliefs. But at the time he was writing *Pilgrim's Progress*, enforcement of the penal code against the Nonconformists had been somewhat relaxed. The power of the authorities had been temporarily curbed. The "lions" had been put in chains. They could still roar at Nonconformists, but if the latter watched their step in walking a straight line along the middle of the path, they could pass safely between the lions.

SECTION 5

Valley of Humiliation and Valley of the Shadow of Death

Summary

Just beyond Palace Beautiful lies the Valley of Humiliation. Christian has scarcely entered it when he sees coming toward him a "foul fiend" named Apollyon—a hideous monster with scales like a fish, wings like a dragon, feet like a bear, mouth like a lion; fire and smoke pour out of a hole in his belly. The monster asks Christian: "Whence come you, and whither are you bound?"

When Christian replies that he is coming from the City of Destruction and bound for the City of Zion, Apollyon points out that he is the prince and god of the City of Destruction and all surrounding territory, that Christian is therefore one of his subjects and owes him obedience, that he should obey his command and turn around and go home. Christian refuses, announcing his intention of continuing "in the King's highway, the way of holiness." With that, Apollyon blocks the path and lets fly at Christian with a flaming dart, which Christian deflects with his shield. But then comes a shower of flaming darts, "thick as hail," inflicting many wounds. Christian's sword is useless to him, for Apollyon stays out of reach as he moves around hurling his darts.

The fight goes on "for above half a day." Toward the end, growing weaker and weaker from loss of blood, Christian has to give way a step or two, at which the monster rushes at him, knocks the sword from his hand, and throws him down, pinning his shoulders to the ground. Thinking each breath will be his last, Christian reaches out a hand, fortunately finds his sword within reach, and plunges it into his tormentor. Apollyon jumps up and staggers back, with Christian after him, hoping to bury his sword in his heart. But the monster escapes by taking to his dragon wings and flying off, threatening to be back again to deal with Christian.

Thanking God for his deliverance by placing his fallen sword within reach, Christian sits down wearily and "there came to him a hand with some of the leaves of the Tree of Life." He applies the leaves to his many wounds, which are "healed immediately." Having eaten the bread and drunk of the bottle given him at Palace Beautiful, he feels sufficiently refreshed to resume his journey, keeping his sword unsheathed in case of another attack, but none comes in this valley.

Christian now enters the Valley of the Shadow of Death, a fearsome place, "a wilderness, a land of deserts and pits, a land of drought and of the shadow of death, a land that no man (but a Christian) passeth through, and where no man dwelt," as the Prophet Jeremiah described it (Jer. 2:6). The path in the valley is very narrow, with a deep, water-filled ditch on one side in which many ("the blind leading the blind") have drowned, and on the other side a great bog, "a very dangerous quag," in which others have perished. In addition, it is quite dark, so that Christian has to walk very slowly and cautiously, often not knowing where his next step will carry him.

Halfway through the valley, he comes to the mouth of Hell, which is spewing forth sparks, flames, and great clouds of smoke. As his sword is of no use to him here, Christian puts it away and takes out another potent weapon, All-prayer (Eph. 6:18), a sort of blanket prayer that covers all kinds of exigencies. Protected by this, Christian goes on a great while, with long fingers of flame reaching after him. Then he hears demons moving all around him, but he cannot see them because of the smoke. He again considers turning back, but rejects the idea. There might be more danger in going back than going forward.

Suddenly, coming from up front, a voice rings out: "Though I walk through the Valley of the Shadow of Death, I will fear no evil, for Thou art with me" (Ps. 23:4). As that cry could have been raised only by a Pilgrim, Christian is "exceeding happy" and hastens forward to see who it is.

Commentary

The foul fiend Apollyon who attacks Christian in the Valley of Humiliation is the Destroyer, the quintessence of evil—"The angel of the bottomless pit whose name in the Hebrew tongue is Abaddon, but in the Greek tongue hath his name Apollyon" (Rev. 9:11). The name also occurs in *St. Bevis of Southampton,* a chivalric romance that was one of Bunyan's favorites.

For the physical characteristics of his giant monster, Bunyan used his imagination but also drew on descriptions of other monsters as given in the Bible and such works as *The Seven Champions of Christendom,* published about a century before and which Bunyan had often read. In the story of St. George and the dragon in that book, the dragon is, like Apollyon, covered with scales, has wings, and breathes fire. Bunyan also drew on the *Seven Champions* for another scene. When St. George is wounded, he is quickly restored by the leaves of a miraculous tree; so are Christian's wounds healed immediately when he applies to them some leaves from the Tree of Life given to him by a mysterious hand.

Some critics have adjudged the Apollyon incident to be a gem of artistic creation. However that may be, this can be said: it is a passage almost free of lengthy theological discourse and expatiation.

Among the hazards Christian meets in the Valley of the Shadow of Death, the deep, water-filled ditch bordering one side of the narrow path is error in belief, into which the blind lead the blind. The quagmire on the other side is carnal sin, in which so many get mired down. Thanks to the magic of All-prayer, Christian gets safely through the valley and hastens to see who it was that raised the cry he heard in the distance.

SECTION 6

Faithful

Summary

To his surprise, Christian finds that the cry had been raised by an old friend, Faithful, one of his neighbors in the City of Destruction. Happy in each other's company, they walk along exchanging the news. Faithful tells Christian that his departure had caused quite a stir in the city, with most people denouncing him as a fool. Faithful adds that he wishes Christian had informed him of his intention, in which case he would have accompanied Christian from the start instead of following after him.

Faithful's adventures along the way had been different from Christian's. He had managed to get around the Slough of Despond in which Christian had floundered, but on the path to the Wicket Gate had been accosted by one Wanton, a woman with a very flattering tongue. She had tried hard to induce him to turn aside with her, promising him "all carnal and fleshly content." But he closed his eyes to her bewitching looks, and walked on.

At the foot of Difficulty Hill, he met a very aged man by the name of Adam the First, who lived in the town of Deceit. Adam invited Faithful to come live with him, saying that his house was "maintained with all the dainties in the world," and that he had three beautiful daughters:

Lust of the Flesh, Lust of the Eyes, and Pride of Life (1 John 2:16). Faithful might marry one of these—or all of them if he so desired—and become his heir. Faithful was "somewhat inclinable" at first but, thinking better of it, went on, with old Adam cursing and reviling him.

Ascending Difficulty Hill as far as the arbor—the very place where he had lost his Roll, Christian interjects—Faithful looked behind and there was someone coming after him, "swift as the wind." Overtaking Faithful, he knocked him down. When Faithful got up, he was knocked down again, and then again. "That man that overtook you was Moses," says Christian, and he "spareth none, neither knoweth he how to show mercy to those that transgress his law." Under the harsh Mosaic Code he was punishing Faithful for having so much as looked at Wanton and for "secretly inclining to Adam the First."

Faithful had not stopped at Palace Beautiful as Christian had, which explained why he had come to be ahead of him on the Holy Way. Traversing the Valley of Humiliation, he had not encountered Apollyon, who was perhaps nursing the wound given him by Christian, but he had met Discontent and another named Shame. The latter argued the view that religion was a "pitiful low sneaking business.... that it was a shame to sit whining and mourning under a sermon, and a shame to come sighing and groaning home." The mighty, rich, and wise did not do that. He had noted that Pilgrims were chiefly men of "base and low estate and condition," having no bravery of spirit nor any understanding of "natural science." Faithful was somewhat taken aback by this, but consoled himself with the thought that what men most esteem is abominated by God, and that "what God says is best, though all the men in the world are against it."

As Christian and Faithful go on walking and talking, they see a tall man, "something more comely at a distance than at hand." When he says he is bound for the heavenly country, Faithful invites him to join them, which is a mistake. Christian soon recognizes the man as Talkative, son of Say-well, of Prating Row, and warns Faithful not to be taken in by him, for "notwithstanding his fine tongue, he is but a sorry scrub.... this man is for any company and for any talk; as he talketh now with you, so will he talk when he is on the ale-bench. And the more drink he hath in his crown, the more of these things he hath in his mouth. Religion hath no place in his heart, or house or conversation; all he hath lieth in his tongue, and his religion is to make a noise therewith." After many long arguments in which Christian and Faithful assail his views, Talkative decides they are peevish men "not fit to be discoursed with," and goes off; "and good riddance," says Christian.

Farther on, Faithful chances to look back and sees someone coming toward them. It is their good friend Evangelist, who asks how they have fared in their journey. In turn, they ask him what they may expect to meet up ahead. There will be tribulations, he answers, for tribulations mark the way to Heaven. They would soon come to a town where they would be attacked by enemies. One or both of them might be killed. "But be you faithful unto death, and the King will give you a crown of life," Evangelist assures them.

Commentary

Until Bunyan brings Faithful on the scene, Christian has faced his major adventures alone. Now he has a good companion at last. Other Pilgrims met along the way have been a sorry lot, Pliant, Formalist, Hypocrisy, Simple, Presumptuous, Timorous, and Mistrust, among others. Christian is overjoyed to meet with an old and trusted friend, a proper Pilgrim, with whom he can discourse at length on the contrast between the miseries of this world and the eternal bliss that awaits the Elect in the Celestial City. Bunyan makes the most of this opportunity for an extended dialogue on the awful mysteries of the Faith.

As a character, Faithful can scarcely be distinguished from Christian, except that he is a bit more naive. Spiritually, they are twins. They see eye to eye on all important matters. The introduction of Faithful also enables Bunyan to describe more of the temptations and perils that beset the Holy Way, for Faithful has met adventures other than Christian's; his near seduction by Madame Wanton and by old Adam ("the carnal spirit") with his three lusty daughters; his merciless beating by Moses, who would have killed him, Faithful is sure, "but that one came by and bid him forbear," his rescuer being the Lord, whom Faithful recognized on perceiving "the holes in his hands and in his side" (the scars of the Crucifixion); his meeting with Discontent and with "that bold villain" Shame, who objected that all religion was "an unmanly thing," that it was "a shame to sit whining and mourning under a sermon when a man, if he is wise, should be out making a place for himself in the world.

One of the more interesting passages in the book is the long involved argument that ensures when Christian and Faithful overtake Talkative and invite him to join them. Their new acquaintance is well named, for he is always ready, as he himself says, to "talk of things heavenly or things earthly, things moral or things evangelical, things sacred or things profane, things past or things to come, things foreign or things at home, things more essential or things circumstantial, provided that all be done to our profit."

Talkative is one of the few characters whom Bunyan endows with any physical features. The others are abstractions characterized solely by their names, such as Hypocrisy, or Evangelist, or Mr. Worldly Wiseman. Talkative, we are told, "is a tall man and something more comely at a distance than at hand." Faithful is quite taken with Talkative at first, finding him "a very pretty fellow," but Christian disagrees, saying that the first impression made by Talkative reminds him of the "work of the painter whose pictures show best at a distance, but very near more unpleasing."

The ever plausible Talkative seems to have bothered Bunyan quite a bit, for he was at great pains to tear him down and prove that, "notwithstanding his fine tongue, he is but a very sorry fellow.... a sounding brass and tinkling cymbal." Christian and Faithful finally quarrel with Talkative about whether salvation is won by Grace, or by Works. As Talkative is not a doer, he has not much faith in Works; everything depends upon Grace. When Christian and Faithful attack him as a dissembling Christian and liken him to a whore, Talkative goes off in a huff, dismissing his questioners as "not fit to be discoursed with." Nothing more is heard of Talkative.

Still keeping watch over the Pilgrims and their progress, Evangelist suddenly appears once again, this time to warn Christian and Faithful—and the reader—that there is danger ahead, that tragedy is impending, that one or the other of them may be killed. But Evangelist has a comforting word and assurance. The one who gets killed "will have the better of his fellow." As a Christian martyr, he will the sooner get to Heaven and be spared "the many miseries the other will meet with in the rest of his journey."

SECTION 7

Vanity Fair

Summary

Emerging from the wilderness, Christian and Faithful see before them a town they must enter because the Holy Way passes through it. It is an ancient town named Vanity Fair, where, all year round, such merchandise is bought and sold "as houses, lands, trades, places, honors, preferments, titles, countries, kingdoms, lusts, pleasures, and delights of all sorts, as whores, bawds, wives, husbands, children, masters, servants, lives, blood, bodies, souls, silver, gold, pearls, precious stones, and what not." At all times, one can see "jugglings, cheats, games, plays, fools, apes, knaves, rogues, and that of all sorts," as well as, "and that for nothing, thefts, murders, adulteries, false-swearers, and that of a blood-red color."

Entering the town, the two Pilgrims cause quite a stir. Their dress is different from that of the townspeople, and they speak a language ("the language of Canaan") that is not understood. They are plainly "outlandish men" (foreigners), and are put down as fools or "bedlams" (madmen). But what particularly irks the townspeople is their attitude toward the goods displayed at the fair. When called to look at them, they turn away, putting their fingers in their ears and crying out, "Turn away mine eyes from beholding vanity" (Ps. 119:37). When mockingly asked what they might be interested in buying, they "gravely" reply, "We buy the Truth" (Prov. 23:23). A crowd gathers to taunt and revile them, "some calling upon others to smite them," which leads to a great hubbub and the arrest of the Pilgrims for disturbing the peace. After being questioned, they are severely beaten and locked up in an iron cage to be made a spectacle to the multitude, being for some time "the objects of any man's sport, or malice, or revenge."

Under these trying circumstances, Christian and Faithful conduct themselves so "very wisely and soberly" that some of the townspeople begin to sympathize with them and urge their release. This splits the town into two factions which soon clash in the streets, creating another hubbub. The prisoners, though they have done nothing, are held responsible for this, too, and the authorities decide to bring them to trial on charges that they are "enemies to and disturbers of their trade; that they have made commotions and divisions in the town, and had won a party to their own most dangerous opinions in contempt of the law of their prince."

Faithful is the first to be called before the judge, Lord Hate-good. When allowed to speak in his own defense, he declares himself to be a man of peace, bound on an innocent journey to the Celestial City; as for the prince of the place, "since he is Beelzebub, the enemy of our Lord, I defy him and all his angels."

To testify against him, three witnesses are brought forward—Envy, Superstition, and Pickthank. Swearing falsely, Envy testifies that he has long known Faithful, that he has always been a troublemaker, persistently denouncing the laws and customs of the town; Superstition, that he had heard Faithful say that all in Vanity Fair were damned because their "religion was naught"; Pickthank, that he was well acquainted with the defendant, who railed continuously against "our noble Prince Beelzebub and...his honorable friends,...Lord Old Man, Lord Carnal Delight, Lord Luxurious, Lord Desire of Vainglory, my old Lord Lechery, Sir Having Greedy, with all the rest of our nobility." Turning toward Lord Hate-good, he adds that Faithful "hath not been afraid to rail on you, my Lord, who are now appointed to be his judge, calling you an ungodly villain, with many other such-like vilifying terms." The jury, having heard the false witnesses and Faithful's reply, retires to discuss what should be done.

"I see clearly that this man is a heretic," says Mr. Blind-man, foreman of the jury.

"Away with such a fellow from this earth," cries Mr. No-good; Mr. Malice, Mr. Love-lust, and Mr. Live-loose agree.

"Hang him, hang him!" exclaims Mr. Heady.

"A sorry scrub," says Mr. High-mind.

"Hanging is too good for him," Mr. Cruelty insists.

After Mr. Liar and other jurors have expressed similar views. Mr. Implacable sums up: "Let us forthwith bring him in guilty of death."

Judge Hate-good is only too happy to order that Faithful be executed in accord with the laws of the land. He is first scourged, "then they buffeted him, then they lanced his flesh with knives; after that they stoned him with stones, then pricked him with their swords and, last of all, they burned him to ashes at the stake. Thus came Faithful to his end." But this was only his earthly end, as Evangelist had prophesied. For unseen by any, "there stood behind the multitude a chariot and a couple of horses, waiting for Faithful, who (so soon as his adversaries had dispatched him) was taken up into it and straightway was carried up through the clouds,...the nearest way to the Celestial City."

For some unexplained reason, Christian is not brought to trial and, after a time, "escapes" and is on his way again – but not alone, for he is joined by Hopeful, a native of Vanity Fair, who had been so impressed by the Pilgrims' words and behavior during their sufferings that he decided to become a Pilgrim himself. And many more in Vanity Fair would follow his path in due time, Hopeful tells Christian, who is pleased to have helped break the power of Beelzebub.

Christian and his new companion have not gone very far when they catch up with a man known as By-ends, from the town of Fair-speech. His is a nickname, given to him because he is shifty, always with an eye out for a good bargain, a "by-end." Fair-speech is a wealthy place, and By-ends boasts of his fine connections there. His wife is the daughter of Lady Feigning, and he is on the best of terms with "my Lord Turn-about, my Lord Time-server,...also Mr. Smooth-man, Mr. Facing-both-ways, Mr. Anything; and the parson of our parish, Mr. Two-tongues,... my mother's own brother by father's side."

Questioned about his beliefs, By-ends replies; " 'Tis true we somewhat differ in religion from those of the stricter sort, yet but in two small points: First, we never strive against wind or tide; secondly, we are always most zealous when religion goes in his silver slippers; we love much to walk with him in the street if the sun shines, and the people applaud him."

Christian and Hopeful tell him that if he wants to go along with them, he must strive against wind and tide, and "own religion in his rags, as well as when in his silver slippers, and stand by him, too, when bound in irons." Saying that he will not desert his old principles, "since they are harmless and profitable," By-ends drops behind and there meets three old friends, Mr. Hold-the-World, Mr. Money-love, and Mr. Save-all. All of them had been students of "one Mr. Gripe-man, a schoolmaster in Love-gain,...in the county of Coveting," who had "taught them the art of getting either by violence, cozenage, flattery, lying, or by putting on a guise of religion." They were such apt pupils that "they could, each of them, have kept such a school themselves."

Discussing By-ends' sin in making "religion a stalking-horse to get and enjoy the world"—the sin of heathens, "the hypocritical Pharisees" "Judas the devil," "Simon the witch," and others—Christian and Hopeful come to a "delicate plain" called Ease, where they do not stop, and go on to "a little hill called Lucre, and in that hill a silver mine." A certain Demas appears and invites them to come over, saying that with a little digging, they can richly provide for themselves. Hopeful suggests having a look, but Christian objects. As they go on their way, they look behind and see By-ends and his friends accept Demas' invitation and turn off toward the silver mine. "Now whether they fell into the pit by looking over the brink thereof, or whether they went down to dig, or whether they were smothered by the damps that commonly arise," Christian and Hopeful never knew, but the By-ends' party they never saw again on the Holy Way.

Commentary

In describing Vanity Fair, Bunyan had only to call to mind what he had seen at small annual county fairs and particularly at the large and renowned year-round fair held at Stourbridge, near Cambridge. Here, as a contemporary noted, "the shops or booths are built in rows like streets, having each its name: as Garlick Row, Booksellers' Row, Cook Row, etc. Here are all sorts of traders who sell by wholesale or retail.... Here is a court of justice [a "Court of Piepowder," from *Pieds Pouldreux*, dusty feet] open from morning till night.... Here are also taverns, coffee-houses, and eating-houses in great plenty.... These mercantile fairs are very injurious to morals."

Similarly at Vanity Fair, as Bunyan depicts it, "there are the several rows and streets under their proper names.... Here is the Britain Row, the French Row, the Italian Row, the Spanish Row, the German Row.... But as in other fairs, some one commodity is as the chief of all the fair, so the ware of Rome [the Roman Catholic Church] and her merchandise is greatly promoted in this fair. Only our English nation, with some others, have taken a dislike thereat."

In this last paragraph, out of his deep Protestant aversion to the Roman Church and his desire to make a point against it, Bunyan gets a bit mixed up about the character of Vanity Fair. Beelzebub, prince of the fair, is bent on destroying all Christians, no matter what their creed, and it is therefore quite out of character to represent him as allowing the "ware of Rome" to be "greatly promoted" at his fair. Subconsciously, Bunyan was equating the pope with Beelzebub, which was doctrinaire and un-Christian. It should be added, however, that Bunyan, for his day, was far more tolerant than most preachers of the Word. He excommunicated, so to speak, only Roman Catholics and Quakers, the latter because they often heckled him when he was preaching on a village green.

When Bunyan came to portraying Lord Hate-good, the arbitrary judge at Faithful's trial, he no doubt had in mind Sir John Kelyne and the other judges who had kept him in jail for so many years. He could present the procedures of the trial realistically out of his own experience as a defendant. Bunyan's use of realistic detail here and throughout the book sharpens his allegory. As pointed out by the novelist C. S. Lewis, it is an "error to suppose that in an allegory the author is 'really' talking about the thing that symbolizes; the very essence of the art is to talk about both."

The introduction of Hopeful, the refugee from Vanity Fair, enables Bunyan to draw a moral: "Thus one died to make testimony to the truth, and another rises out of his ashes to be a companion with Christian in his pilgrimage." With Hopeful, Christian does not raise the point, as he did with others, that he should have come in at the Wicket Gate, the only proper entrance to the Holy Way. It should also be noted that Hopeful, quite ignorant of Christianity as one of Beelzebub's subjects, proves to be a remarkably apt convert. He is immediately talking the "mysteries" of Christian doctrine with ease, quoting from the Bible and alluding to it almost as learnedly as Christian.

After Vanity Fair, the long silver mine incident, involving By-ends and his friends, comes as something of an anticlimax. Both deal with the evils of "lucre," and Vanity Fair makes the point better.

SECTION 8

By-Path Meadow and Doubting Castle

Summary

Having passed a pillar of salt in the shape of a woman, upon which is written "Remember Lot's wife," Christian and Hopeful come to a very pleasant river, "which David the King called 'the river of God,' but John called 'the river of the water of life' " (Ps. 65:9; Rev. 22, 1-3; Ezek. 47). It is lined with fruit trees and beautiful meadows bright with lilies and other flowers. Drinking the Water of Life, the weary Pilgrims are greatly refreshed and remain here for several days, picking fruit and sleeping in the meadows.

Moving on, they find that the Holy Way runs along the river bank for a time, but then it veers off onto rough round which is very hard on their sore feet. They are "much discouraged" until they come to another meadow, "and a stile to go over into it, and that meadow is called By-path Meadow." Suggesting that the going might be easier in the meadow, Christian climbs over the stile* to have a look. Finding a path there going their way, he persuades Hopeful that they should take it.

Making good time in By-path Meadow, which is "very easy for their feet," they catch up with another Pilgrim, by the name of Vain-confidence.

*Common in the English countryside, a stile is a set of steps, usually made of wood but sometimes of stone, an easy way of getting over a high wall or fence.

Assuring them that he knows the way, their new acquaintance starts out ahead and tells them to follow him. As it is now night and very dark, they soon lose sight of him and continue on until they hear a loud cry and a heavy thud. Creeping forward, they find that Vain-confidence has been killed by falling into a deep pit dug "by the prince of those grounds to catch vainglorious fools withal."

Christian and Hopeful turn back, scarcely knowing where they are, meeting great difficulties. It is not only dark, but now it begins to rain, with terrible lightning and thunder. The water rises till they are "like to have been drowned nine or ten times." Despairing of finding the stile that night, they lie down in the meadow to sleep.

In the morning they are surprised and seized by the owner of the meadow, Giant Despair. Charging them with trespassing, he drags them to his stronghold, Doubting Castle, and throws them into a "nasty and stinking" dungeon. Here they lie for four days "without one bit of bread, or drop of drink, or light, or any to ask how they did." Giant Despair finally appears and beats them with a crabtree cudgel until they can scarcely roll over on the floor.

When he talks with his wife Diffidence about what to do with the prisoners, she suggests that he might save himself some exertion if he did not kill the prisoners himself but counseled them to take their own lives. He does this, telling them that, since they are going to die anyhow and have their bodies thrown on the heap of human bones and skulls behind the castle, they might prefer to do away with themselves, "either with knife, halter, or poison." When his counsel is rejected, he rushes at the Pilgrims to kill them then and there. But he is subject to fits, it appears, and he is seized with one now, temporarily losing the use of his hands, so he withdraws, leaving Christian and Hopeful to ponder their dilemma.

Christian is uncertain about what to do. For his part, Hopeful rules out suicide; "for one to kill himself is to kill body and soul at once," a more heinous sin than murder of another. Suicide would forever bar them from entering the heavenly Jerusalem. Perhaps their case is not so desperate, Hopeful suggests. Maybe the giant will die, or forget to lock the dungeon doors, or be permanently disabled by one of his fits.

Toward evening, the giant appears in the dungeon again and, finding that the prisoners have not taken his advice, rages against them so furiously and threatens them with such dire punishment that Christian swoons. When the latter comes to, he again contemplates suicide. Hopeful urges a little more patience, pointing out that Christian had driven off Apollyon, passed safely through the Valley of the Shadow of Death, and managed to escape from Vanity Fair. "Well, on Saturday about midnight," they begin to pray and continue until almost daybreak. Suddenly, Christian cries out:

"What a fool am I, thus to lie in a stinking dungeon, when I may as well walk at liberty? I have a key in my bosom called Promise that will (I am persuaded) open any lock in Doubting Castle."

"That's good news," says Hopeful. "Good brother, pluck it out of thy bosom and try."

They try it on the dungeon door, which opens with ease, as do other doors in the castle. Outside, they try it on a big iron gate, which finally opens, though the lock "went damnable hard." As they push the big gate open, its rusty hinges creak so loudly that Giant Despair is awakened. Jumping up, he is dressing to pursue the prisoners when he suffers another fit and has to go back to bed.

Running with desperate speed, Christian and Hopeful finally find the stile by which they entered By-path Meadow, climb over it, and are once again on the King's highway. Before going on, they decide to erect a pillar, on the side of which they engrave a warning: "Over this stile is the way to Doubting Castle, which is kept by Giant Despair, who despiseth the King of the Celestial Country, and seeks to destroy his holy Pilgrims."

Commentary

On first coming to the pillar of salt in the form of a woman, neither Christian nor Hopeful can make anything of it. Then Hopeful sees some writing on the forehead of the woman, written "in an unusual hand." As he is no scholar, he calls Christian, who is "learned...and after a little laying of letters together," makes out the inscription, "Remember Lot's wife." The pillar of salt, they now perceive, is that into which Lot's wife was turned "for her looking back with a covetous heart when she was going from Sodom for safety" (Gen. 19:26).

This "sudden and amazing sight," they agree, "came opportunely to us after the invitation which Demas gave us to come over to view the Hill Lucre. And had we gone over,... we had been made ourselves like this woman, a spectacle for those that shall come after to behold.... This ministereth occasion to us to thank God, to fear before him, and always to remember Lot's wife." Like so many of the day, Bunyan may have believed that the pillar was still to be seen, as reported several centuries earlier in the fantastical *Travels of Sir John Mandeville*, who wrote: "at the right side of the Dead Sea the wife of Lot still stands in likeness of a salt stone."

The incidents in the By-path Meadow and Doubting Castle episode are among the more vivid and dramatic in the book, and are used to symbolize many things and to point a number of moral lessons, some of which are obvious. For one thing, the path to Heaven is straight and narrow and, no matter how rough the going, must be followed. There is no easy bypass, as Christian and Hopeful discover in seeking to favor their sore tired feet—a "carnal" self-indulgence that leads them almost to death not once but several times.

In By-path Meadow, they meet Vain-confidence (at the moment, there is more than a bit of vain confidence in them), and they decide to follow him as he leads the way in the dark. Except that they were less "vainglorious" than he, they might have taken the lead and in the dark stumbled into the deep pit that took his life.

As they turn back, hoping to find the stile by which they entered By-path Meadow, they are assaulted by the elements as if divinely ordered to teach them a lesson. With lightning flashing and thunder rolling "in a very dreadful manner," the rain comes down in torrents, rapidly creating flood waters in which they are almost drowned "nine or ten times." Despairing of finding their way on such a stormy night, they lie down to sleep in the meadow, only to be seized in the morning by Giant Despair and thrown into the dungeon at Doubting Castle, where they are starved and mercilessly beaten.

The imprisonment in Doubting Castle symbolizes a period of extreme spiritual distress on the part of the two Pilgrims. They are locked up by their own fears and doubts. Can they keep the Faith as it should be kept? Are they among those predestined for salvation? Giant Despair represents the despair in their own hearts, and the giant's hold is broken as soon as Christian remembers that he is carrying a key that will, he is persuaded, "open any lock in Doubting Castle," as proves to be the case. The key is "called Promise," a belief in the assurance that a true Christian will be forgiven his trespasses and errors, if minor, and not be rejected at the Celestial Gate.

It is strange and rather amusing that such an overpowering creature as Giant Despair should suffer from fits which come on "sometimes in sunshine weather" and leave him temporarily withouse use of his hands. There is a bit of symbolism here. Black despair loses its grip when brought out into the sunshine, into the light. Providentially for Christian and Hopeful, the author puts Giant Despair into fits at just the right time, when he is about to bash in the skulls of the two Pilgrims with his crabtree cudgel, and when he falls back into bed when getting up to pursue the escaping prisoners.

What with Christian's miraculous escapes from death at the hands of Apollyon, in the hellish Valley of the Shadow of Death, in Vanity Fair, and then in Doubting Castle, the story line begins to call to mind the script of some old-time movie serial, like "The Perils of Pauline," in which the heroine is tied across a railroad track and the locomotive of a huge train comes thundering down on her, within a few feet of her, when an unseen hand reaches out and saves her for another hairbreadth rescue in next week's serial.

SECTION 9

Delectable Mountains

Summary

Still talking of the perils they have just passed through safely, thanks to God, Christian and Hopeful come to the Delectable Mountains, which Christian had seen in the distance from the roof of Palace Beautiful. The mountains are indeed delectable, with gardens and orchards, vineyards and fountains of water. They drink and wash in the waters, "freely eat of the vineyards," and feel much refreshed. Climbing upward, they come upon four shepherds—Knowledge, Experience, Watchful, and Sincere—who welcome them and invite them to their tents for supper and to spend the night. "These mountains are Immanuel's Land," the shepherds explain, "and they are within sight of his city; and the sheep also are his, and he laid down his life for them."

Next morning, the shepherds escort their guests around the mountains to show them some of the wonders of the place, taking them first to the top of a hill called Error. On the far side of the hill is a high cliff. Peering over, Christian and Hopeful see at the bottom of it some men dashed all to pieces. These men, so they are told, were some of those who, like the Quakers, err in having no faith in the resurrection of the body. The bodies of those at the foot of the cliff would remain forever unburied as an "example to others to take heed how they clamber too high, or how they come too near the brink of this mountain."

Having been taken to the top of another mountain, named Caution, the Pilgrims are led into a hollow where there is a door in the side of a hill. When the door is opened, they are invited to look in, which they do and are terrified. Inside, it is very dark and smoky, smelling of brimstone. They can hear the noise of fire and a cry of some tormented. "This is a by-way to Hell," Christian is told when he inquires, "a way that hypocrites go in at; namely, such as sell their birthright, with Esau; such as sell their Master, with Judas...."

The Pilgrims are next taken to the top of a very high hill, named Clear, where the shepherds hand them a "perspective glass" (telescope) and tell them that if they have skill in using it, they will be able to see the gates of the Celestial City. Christian and Hopeful have a look but as their hands are shaking, they cannot see clearly, though they think they see "something like the gate, and also some of the glory of the place." As the Pilgrims prepare to depart, the shepherds give them written instructions on how to go on the way ahead, and what to avoid. Let them beware of the Flatterer, and be sure not to sleep on the Enchanted Ground.

Beyond the mountains, the Holy Way is joined by a little crooked lane which comes down from the country of Conceit. Just as the Pilgrims reach this point, there comes swinging down the lane "a very brisk lad" to whom Bunyan gives the name Ignorance. He, too, is bound for the Celestial City. Why had he not come in at the Wicket Gate? Christian wants to know. And what reason had he to believe that if he ever got to the Celestial Gate, it would be opened for him? Because he has always led a good life and knows God's will, Ignorance replies: "I pray, fast, pay tithes, and give alms." When Christian and Hopeful argue that this is not enough, Ignorance tells them to mind their own business: "be content to follow the religion of your country, and I will follow the religion of mine. I hope all will be well."

Finding him a man "wise in his own conceit" and not worth talking to, Christian and Hopeful push ahead and soon enter a very dark lane, where they see a man who has been bound with seven strong cords by seven devils; they are carrying him back to throw him through the door to Hell in the Delectable Mountains. Christian recognizes the man as one Turn-away, "a wanton professor and damnable apostate," and is reminded of a story he once heard about one Little-faith, from the town of Sincere.

While Christian is relating to Hopeful the story he had heard about Little-faith and his tribulations, they come to a fork in the path. One fork seems to lead as straight as the other in the direction they want to go. As they stand wondering which path to take, they are approached by a man "black of flesh, but covered with a very light robe." He is bound for the Celestial City himself, the man says, and as he knows the right way, they should follow him, which they do. He leads them in a circular course and finally into a great net in which they become helplessly entangled; "and with that, the white robe fell off the black man's back," and the Pilgrims recognize that they have been seduced by Flatterer, "a false apostle that hath transformed himself into an angel of light." After a time, a Shining One appears, tears the net open, frees the prisoners, and then begins to question them:

Had not the shepherds on the Delectable Mountains given them "a note of direction for the way?"

"Yes."

"Did you, when you were at a stand, pluck out and read your note?"

"No."

"Why?"

"We forgot."

"Did not the shepherds bid you beware of the Flatterer?"

"Yes. But we did not imagine that this fine-spoken man had been he."

The Shining One orders Christian and Hopeful to lie down and with the small-cord whip he is carrying, lays it on them and chastens "them sore, to teach them the good way wherein they should walk." Thanking him "for all his kindness," promising to reform, the Pilgrims are up again and on their way till they see someome coming toward them, "with his back toward Zion." They stop to talk with this man, who turns out to be Atheist. When he learns of their hopes and plans, he starts laughing, saying that they will have only their pains for their travel.

"Do you think we shall not be received?" asks Christian.

"Received! There is no such place as you dream of in all this world."

"But there is in the world to come."

Atheist replies that he had once heard this and believed it, and had set out to discover if it were true. He had spent twenty years searching for the Celestial City and had not found it anywhere. It was a mirage. Laughing again at their dreams, Atheist continues on his way toward home, leaving the Pilgrims deeply shocked. "What! no Mount Zion!" exclaims Hopeful. But had they not seen the gate of the city from the Delectable Mountains? Were they not now to walk by Faith (2 Cor. 5:7)? And they had better be getting along, Hopeful adds, "lest the man with the whip overtakes us again."

Going on, they come to a place where Hopeful, becoming very drowsy, wants to lie down and take a nap. By no means, says Christian. This is the Enchanted Ground the shepherds had warned them about. Those who fall asleep here never wake up. "Let us watch and be sober" (1 Thes. 5:6) and "to prevent drowsiness, let us fall into good discourse." (Their "good discourse" goes on and on, being a sermon in the form of a duet, with Christian sounding one note and Hopeful chiming in to sound another. As none of this advances the story of the pilgrimage one bit, the long passage is omitted in most modern editions of the book.)

The "good discourse" is interrupted when Hopeful happens to look back and sees Ignorance coming up behind them. They stop to wait for him:

"How stands it between God and your soul now?" Christian greets him.

"I hope well, for I am always full of good motions that come into my mind to comfort me as I walk."

"What good motions?"

Well, says Ignorance, he keeps thinking of God and Heaven. When Christian remarks, "So do the devils and damned souls," Ignorance objects that his case is quite different, for he not only thinks of God and Heaven constantly, but desires them and has left all for them. Saying he doubts this, Christian asks what reason he has to suppose that he has given up everything in his desire to go to Heaven. Because his heart tells him so, answers Ignorance, to which Christian tartly replies: "He that trusts his own heart is a fool....Except the Word of God beareth witness in this matter, other testimony is of no value."

As Christian and Hopeful go on catechizing Ignorance as if he were a small boy, the latter understandably becomes somewhat annoyed and declares that their notions about the correct meaning of the Word are "but the fruit of distracted brains," as shown by their belief in revelations. This provokes Hopeful to exclaim: "Why man! Christ is so hid in God from the natural apprehensions of all flesh that he cannot by any man be savingly known unless God the Father reveals him to them."

"That is your Faith, but not mine," says Ignorance. "Yet mine, I doubt not, is as good as yours, though I have not in my head so many whimsies as you." Giving up on Ignorance, who drops behind again, Christian and Hopeful resume their "good discourse."

Commentary

After the rigors endured by the Pilgrims on their ill-advised excursion into By-path Meadow and the tortures they suffered in the Doubting Castle dungeon, the Delectable Mountains present a quiet pastoral scene, with the shepherds – Knowledge, Experience, Watchful, and Sincere – lovingly watching over the sheep and lambs of the Lord. In telling his story, Bunyan generally follows the pattern of presenting scenes of peace, harmony, and spiritual comfort after incidents involving danger, conflict, and physical violence: after the Slough of Despond, Interpreter's House; after Difficulty Hill, Palace Beautiful; after the horrors of Vanity Fair, the Delectable Mountains.

But even on the Delectable Mountains there are admonitory signs of danger of which Christian and Hopeful are made aware by being shown them: Error Hill with its high cliff over which many Pilgrims have tumbled to their deaths after being led there by erroneous doctrines; Caution Hill, from which the two Pilgrims see blind men stumbling over tombs; the door to Hell in a hillside, a sight that terrifies the Pilgrims and leaves them with their hands shaking so violently that they cannot properly handle the "perspective glass" through which they were to get a glimpse of the Celestial Gate, though "they thought they saw something like a Gate." Hell is never long out of Bunyan's thoughts; as will be seen, he even places a door to Hell right next to the Celestial City.

The character of Ignorance, the "very brisk lad" from the country of Conceit, is an interesting one. Though Bunyan disapproves of him, and finally assigns him to Hell, Ignorance is presented rather sympathetically. He is obviously a lad of good intentions; he wants to go to Heaven and is determined to get there. His only fault is that he is deficient in theology, that he does not share what he calls the whimsical notions of Christian and Hopeful about revelations and other recondite matters. To judge from their long conversations with him, Christian and Hopeful think that Ignorance is not beyond redemption. But as he refuses to see the "Light," he is given up as damned. Ignorance bothers Bunyan quite a lot, for he devotes the last paragraph of his book to him.

Christian and Hopeful then meet Flatterer. Why he is so named is a mystery. He uses no flattery at all when he says simply, "follow me," and leads them in a circle and into a net from which they have to be rescued, providentially, by a Shining One. The latter beats them roundly with a whip for forgetting to read the instructions given them by the shepherds to warn them against Flatterer and others eager to lead them astray. Depicted as a black man in a white robe, Flatterer is Satan in one of his disguises.

Christian and Hopeful next meet Atheist coming down the path on his way home after a long pilgrimage. Bunyan's picture of Atheist is rather surprising. One would expect him to be presented as a dour and belligerent man, opinionated and argumentative, altogether an unpleasant character. Nothing of the kind; he turns out to be a rather jolly fellow, and very matter of fact. When he learns of the Pilgrims' hoped-for destination, he breaks out in a loud laugh.

"I laugh to see what ignorant persons you are, to take upon you so tedious a journey"—and all for nothing. There is no such place as the Celestial City on Mount Zion. He had once believed there was, he says, and had set out to find it. For twenty years he had been journeying here, there, and everywhere, and could not find it, nor any trace of it, nor any clue as to where it might be. It was all a dream. So now, Atheist adds, "I am going back again and will refresh myself with the things that I then cast away for hopes of that which I see is not." The Pilgrims are greatly shaken up by this, not only by what Atheist has said, but by its cool matter-of-factness.

"What! no Mount Zion!" exclaims Hopeful, turning toward Christian. But there must be, he argues. It says so in the Book. They should continue as they have been doing, "walking by Faith." As they hurry off, Atheist goes his way, "laughing at them."

It may or may not be symbolic, but Atheist is the only one in the story who laughs and seems to be content. The other characters are so serious and solemn, and so constantly apprehensive. To hazard a speculation here, it would seem from the characterization of Atheist and the whole tone of the passage that Bunyan had more respect and even affection for the downright non-believer than for those who use professions of Faith to cloak their pursuit of very earthly aims and ambitions.

SECTION 10

Beulah Land, Dark River, and Celestial City

Summary

Leaving the Enchanted Ground and terminating their discourse, the Pilgrims enter "a delightful land, the country of Beulah" (Isa. 62:4; Song of Sol. 2:10-12). Here the sun "shineth night and day," the air is sweet and pleasant, flowers bloom everywhere, birds sing continually, and "the voice of the turtle is heard in the land." Beulah lies within sight of the Celestial City, "builded of pearls and precious stones.... and pure gold." The reflection of the sun on it is so bright as to be blinding.

Passing orchards, vineyards, and gardens, the Pilgrims meet the Gardener, who tells them that the Lord himself comes down from the city now and again to enjoy a bit of rural peace and beauty, and to rest in one of the arbors. Christian and Hopeful are soon joined by two men dressed in golden raiment and whose faces shine "as the light." Accompanied by these angels, they suddenly come to Dark River, broad and swift. There is no bridge over it, no boat to carry them across, and they are "very much astounded," asking their companions what they should do.

"You must go through, or you cannot come at the gate." Is the water all of a depth? No, they are told, "you shall find it deeper or shallower, as you believe in the King of the place." Crossing the River of Death is a test of Faith. Apprehensively, the Pilgrims wade in and presently Christian cries out: "I sink in deep waters; the billows go over my head; all his waves go over me. Selah.... I shall not see the land that flows with milk and honey."

"Be of good cheer," Hopeful calls out, saying that he has found good footing and will help him. But Christian goes down in "a great darkness and horror" as he recalls all his sins "both since and before he began to be a Pilgrim." Somewhat losing his senses, he begins to see hobgoblins and evil spirits. Hopeful has all he can do "to keep his brother's head above water. Yea, sometimes he would be quite gone down, and then ere a while he would rise up again, half dead." This goes on until Hopeful persuades him that he is not lost, that his faith in Christ will save him, which it does.

Reaching the far bank of the river, the wet and weary Pilgrims find Shining Ones waiting for them. The ascent to the Celestial City is steep, for it stands "on a mighty hill.... higher than the clouds." But the ascent for them is easy because the Shining Ones, taking them by the arms, help them up and because "they had left their mortal garments behind them in the river." As they are climbing, a company of the Heavenly Host comes out to greet them, as well as several of the King's trumpeters, who make the Heavens ring "with melodious noises and loud."

Over the Celestial Gate is written in letters of gold: "Blessed are they that do his Commandments, that they may have right to the Tree of Life and may enter in through the gate into the city." From the parapet above the gate, some notables are looking down—"Enoch, Moses, and Elijah, &c." They direct the Pilgrims to hand in their certificates, which are carried forthwith to the "King of the place" (God). Satisfied after examining their credentials, the Lord orders the gate to be opened so that they "that keepeth Truth may enter in."

With bells pealing joyously, Christian and Hopeful walk into the city and are "transfigured." They are clothed in new raiment that shines like gold. Each is given a golden harp and a gold crown, and they are soon marching along the gold-paved streets with many of the Heavenly Host, some of whom have wings. All are playing their harps and, "without intermission," singing in chorus: "Holy, Holy, Holy, is the Lord"—which is the last seen of Christian and Hopeful in the Paradise they have been seeking.

Not long after the gate was closed behind them, another Pilgram approaches and knocks. It is Ignorance, who has been plodding along behind since Christian and Hopeful walked off and left him. When the keepers of the gate ask him for his certificate, Ignorance fumbles "in his bosom" as if he had a paper and could not find it. When pressed about this, he does not answer. On being informed of this, the King orders several of the Shining Ones to seize Ignorance, bind him hand and foot, carry him to the door to Hell just outside the Celestial City, and throw him through it. On that note the book ends, with the author remarking: "So I awoke, and behold it was a dream."

Bunyan appended to his book four stanzas of rather doggerel verse, of which some lines are these:

Now, reader, I have told my dream to thee.
See if thou canst interpret it to me,
Or to thyself, or neighbor....

Take heed, also that thou be not extreme
In playing with the outside of my dream.

Nor let my figure, or similitude,
Put thee into laughter or a feud.
Leave this for boys and fools; but as for thee,
Do thou the substance of the matter see....

What of my dross thou findest there, be bold
To throw away, but yet preserve the gold....
But if thou shalt cast all away as vain,
I know not but 'twill make me dream again.

Commentary

Some of the symbolism and the specific imagery in the Beulah Land episode is distinctly Freudian. Beulah means "married," and among the other beauties and delights of the land, it is here, so Bunyan tells us, that the "contract between the bride and bridegroom was renewed. Yea, here, as the bridegroom rejoiceth over the bride, so did their God rejoice over them" (Isa. 62:5). Christian is so ravished by the idea that he almost swoons "with desire"; Hopeful has "a fit or two of the same disease." Being quite overcome, they lie down for a while, crying out in ecstasy and longing: "If you see my Beloved, tell him that I am sick of love" (Song of Sol. 5-8).

The happenings at the crossing of the Dark River come as something of a surprise. As safe passage depends on Faith, one would expect that Christian would get across much more easily than Hopeful, who is still something of a novice saint. But it is the other way around. Bunyan wishes to immerse Christian in all his paralyzing doubts again to make his hero's ultimate triumph all the greater. It is Hopeful with his helping hand and reassuring words who keeps Christian afloat in the River of Death till the latter overcomes his misgivings about salvation, glimpses his Redeemer once again, and thereupon walks safely ashore through shallow water.

As the gate swings open to admit Christian and Hopeful to the Celestial City, one is rather surprised and disappointed that Bunyan offers only the briefest glimpse into his solid-gold, jewel-encrusted Heaven. One expects to be shown something more interesting and inspiring than bands of angels with gold crowns walking up and down gold-paved streets playing gold harps and incessantly singing, "Holy, Holy, Holy." Later, in Part II, Bunyan comes back to the subject and tells us a bit more about what life is like on Mount Zion and how well Christian is faring there.

One is surprised also at the way Bunyan concludes his book. One would think it natural and logical for him to end the story with the triumph of Christian and Hopeful in finally attaining their goal and being admitted into the Celestial City to enjoy the beatitudes of eternal life there. Instead, he tacks on a paragraph relating how Ignorance, having made it all the way to the Celestial City, is repulsed there, seized by order of God, and tossed through a door into Hell. This scene obviously pleased Bunyan and afforded him great satisfaction. Otherwise, he would not have used it as the final point in his book.

But a reader with a sense of fair play may not be so pleased. His sympathy is apt to lie with Ignorance. His sudden consignment to Hell seems to be quite arbitrary and heartless. However "ignorant" and erroneous his religious views might appear to Christian and Hopeful, his credentials as a persevering Pilgrim could not be challenged. Over many obstacles, he had plodded along as far as the Pearly Gates. Instead of being turned away there for not having a proper passport, a certificate, such as Bunyan had provided for Christian and Hopeful, it would have been only fair, it seems, that he should have been commended and comforted a bit, and told to apply again when he had corrected his ideological errors. That he should be cast into Hell, in addition, certainly appears to be cruel and unusual punishment for one who only wanted to be an angel.

The verses appended to the narrative are rather touching. Bunyan is afraid that readers may fail to unravel his riddles, that his story may provoke "laughter or a feud." Whatever dross may be found in the tale, the reader should cast away, "but yet preserve the gold."

> But if thou shall cast all away as vain,
> I know not but 'twill make me dream again.

Bunyan did "dream" again, not because his book was cast away, but rather because it quickly became so popular in Puritan circles—in particular, among humble people in town and country—that readers were eager for a sequel.

REVIEW QUESTIONS AND ESSAY TOPICS

1. *The Pilgrim's Progress* is an allegory. What is an allegory? (It might be helpful to look up in a reference work the exact meaning of somewhat related terms, *parable, symbolism, metaphor, fantasy, similitude;* Bunyan described his story as "delivered under the similitude of a dream.")

2. Taking a major incident in the story as an example, show in detail how Bunyan used allegory to sharpen his meaning by making graphic the points he wished to make, by personalizing abstractions.

3. Who is Interpreter? On what clues do you base your opinion?

4. What is the significance of the Cross and the happenings there? What was the "Roll" that the three Shining Ones gave to Christian?

5. What does Palace Beautiful symbolize? What point was Bunyan making in stressing the fact that Faithful, Christian's friend and traveling companion, passed by the palace without stopping there?

6. Review the description of Vanity Fair. What is Bunyan saying here?

7. Why does Bunyan introduce Mr. Talkative? Is he a convincing character or merely a straw man set up as a target for Christian's (that is, Bunyan's) arguments?

8. Is Doubting Castle really a place, or just a state of mind? Or is it both?

9. What do you make of Bunyan's description of the Celestial City and its environs? Would you undertake a long pilgrimage to get there? Why, or why not?

10. It has been said that Christian is Everyman. In what sense, and to what extent, might this be true?

Part II

In 1684, six years after the first edition of *The Pilgrim's Progress,* Bunyan published a sequel. Also called *The Pilgrim's Progress,* it had the same title page except that "Second Part" was added and the descriptive summary was changed to read: "Wherein Is Set Forth the Manner of the Setting Out of Christian's Wife and Children, Their Dangerous Journey and Safe Arrival at the Desired Country." Though issued separately and years apart, the two books are now usually published together in a single volume.

Bunyan begins with a long preface, written in verse and entitled "The Author's Way of Sending Forth His Second Part of *The Pilgrim.*" In this, Bunyan notes with pride and satisfaction the success and widespread influence of his first book:

> In France and Flanders, where men kill each other,
> My Pilgrim is esteemed a brother.
> In Holland, too, 'tis said, as I am told,
> My Pilgrim is with some worth more than gold.
> Highlanders and wild Irish can agree
> My Pilgrim should familiar with them be.
> 'Tis in New England under such advance,
> Receives there so much loving countenance,
> As to be trimmed, new clothed, and decked with gems....
> If thou art nearer home, it will appear
> My Pilgrim knows no ground of shame or fear;
> City and country will him entertain
> With "Welcome Pilgrim." Yea, they can't
> Refrain from smiling....*

Bunyan expresses a hope and a confidence that his story about the Pilgrimage of Christiana and her children, and the people they pick up along the way, will be as well received as his story about Christian. In this, he was disappointed, for his sequel, like so many sequels, was an inferior work, or at least was generally regarded as such by the more devout. And yet, Part II has its points. It tells a story with many more

*Editions of the book were first published in French and Dutch in 1685; in New England, at Boston, in 1681. At the time Bunyan was writing, the ninth edition of his book was coming off the press in London.

human touches than Part I. It is not so epic, insistent, single-minded, having many pleasant diversions and digressions.

SYNOPSIS

Christian's wife, Christiana, misses her husband, and, hearing how well he is doing in Heaven, regrets that she did not go with him when he set out on his pilgrimage, as she had been urged and invited to do. She makes up her mind to follow him after receiving from a visitor a note from the Lord, written "in letters of gold," inviting her to come to the Celestial City. Though her neighbors try to dissuade her, citing the great dangers of such a journey, Christiana sets out from the City of Destruction with her children—four sons—and is joined by Mercy, a comely young woman of the town.

Passing through the Slough of Despond with much less difficulty than Christian encountered, the Pilgrim party comes to the Wicket Gate, the entrance to the Holy Way, the straight and narrow path leading to Mount Zion. Christiana and the children are immediately admitted by the gatekeeper, but Mercy is left outside. Thinking herself abandoned, Mercy swoons. On Christiana's plea, the gatekeeper comes out, helps Mercy to her feet, and leads the party to a pleasant summer parlor, where the Lord soon appears to assure Mercy that she is welcome as a Pilgrim.

Leaving the Wicket Gate, the party is still within sight of it when the women are accosted by two villainous men who try first to seduce them and then to rape them, which results in a "very great scuffle," with the women crying "Murder! murder!" Hearing this, one of those at the Wicket Gate comes running to the rescue and chases away the villains, who escape by leaping over a wall into Satan's garden.

Coming to Interpreter's House, the party is well entertained there and shown the sights, including some that had not been shown to Christian. On the eve of their departure, Interpreter assigns Great-heart, a stout and well-armed Christian soldier, to be their conductor for the rest of the way. Surmounting Difficulty Hill with its many steep ascents, the party approaches the lane leading to Palace Beautiful. Here are two chained lions, as Christian had found. But now there is also a giant, one Grim, or Bloody-man, who emerges from a cave and blocks the way. Great-heart advances, whacks off his head, and leads the party into

Palace Beautiful, which is filled with songs of joy. Christiana and her group like it so well here that, upon being invited, they stay a month, enjoying much feasting and godly discourse with the palace virgins.

During their stay, Mercy is courted by a Mr. Brisk, but he soon jilts her upon discovering that the clothes she is always so busily making are not for sale, not to make money, but to be given away to the poor. Obviously, she would not make a thrifty, prudent housewife. But Mercy will not long remain a maiden, for she is soon "given" in marriage to Christiana's oldest son, Matthew.

Descending from Palace Beautiful into the Valley of Humiliation, where Christian had been attacked and almost killed by the monster Apollyon, Christiana and her party meet with no trouble there, nor much in the Valley of the Shadow of Death, though Great-heart has to drive away some devils and a lion there, and has to slay another giant, one Maul, and take off his head. Going on, the party comes upon an old man asleep under a tree. Recognizing him as a Pilgrim by his clothes, staff, and girdle, they awaken him. He proves to be Old Honest from the Town of Stupidity, on his way to the Celestial City. Joining the party, he directs them to a tavern kept by Gaius, a "very honorable disciple."

The stay at Gaius' Inn, lasting a month or more, is very pleasant. Gaius informs Christiana of her husband's illustrious ancestry. His forebears, it appears, were St. Paul, St. Peter, St. Stephen, and many another ancient prophet, saint, and martyr, including St. Marcus of Arethusa, who "was hanged up in a basket in the sun for the wasps to eat." It is at Gaius' Inn that Mercy is "given" in marriage to Christiana's oldest son, Matthew, and Gaius gives his daughter Phoebe to another son, James.

Here, too, Great-heart gets himself another giant, one Slay-good. He finds the giant rifling the pockets of a captured Pilgrim named Feeble-mind, intending later to eat him. Great-heart takes off the giant's head as another trophy and rescues Feeble-mind, who joins Christiana's party. Another Pilgrim joins her party—Mr. Ready-to-halt, who is so crippled that he has to hobble along on crutches.

Coming to the town of Vanity Fair, where Christian and Faithful had been so harshly treated, Faithful having been burned at the stake there, Great-heart leads the party to the house of a friend, Mnason, a native of the island of Cyprus. There are more marriages here, with Mnason giving daughters to Christiana's two unwedded sons, and

Great-heart goes after another monster, a beast having a dragon's body topped with "seven heads and ten horns." Great-heart does not succeed in taking off the monster's seven heads, but so injures him that everybody expects him to die of his wounds.

When Christiana's party comes to By-path Meadow and Doubting Castle, where Christian and Hopeful had been so pummeled by Giant Despair, Great-heart suggests that it might be a good idea if they took time off to kill the giant and demolish his castle. They do this, taking a week to tear down the castle, bringing back two captured Pilgrims they found in the dungeon—Mr. Despondency and his daughter Much-afraid. These two join the party, which now numbers sixteen, having become so large that it has to walk in column along the straight and narrow path.

The Celestial Mountains are much the same as they were when Christian and Hopeful visited, except that the shepherds have built a palace there, which seems rather incongruous. In any case, there is a palace, so Bunyan tells us, and in its dining room a looking glass that Mercy covets, saying that if it is denied her, she may have a miscarriage. The shepherds happily present her with the marvelous mirror, which held one way, shows "the Prince of Pilgrims himself. . . . the very Crown of Thorns upon his head, . . . the holes in his hands, in his feet, and his side."

Leaving the Delectable Mountains, the Pilgrims come upon a man standing in the road with drawn sword and his face all bloody—Valiant-for-truth, who has just routed three villains who attacked him. Valiant-for-truth joins the party as it proceeds into the Enchanted Ground, where no Pilgrim should rest and sleep if he hopes ever to wake again. Here they find a man kneeling in the roadway, his hands upstretched toward Heaven, praying mightily to God to rescue him from the clutches of a Madam Bubble, who has been persistently trying to seduce him.

The prayerful man, Stand-fast, joins the party as it goes on into the Land of Beulah, where "the sun shineth day and night" and flowers bloom in profusion the year round. Beulah Land, as presented in this part of the book, is sort of a receiving station for those Heaven-bound. Here Pilgrims wait until they are personally summoned to come up to the Celestial City. In her party, Christiana is the first to be summoned, then the others in order, and all wade through the Dark River, the River of Death, and are whisked up to the Celestial Gate in chariots driven by angels—all but Christian's four sons and their pregnant brides, who are left behind to propagate "for the increase of the Church in that place they were for a time."

PRINCIPAL CHARACTERS

(Characters identified for Part I are not listed here.)

Christiana

Christian's wife, who, regretting that she did not go with her husband in the first place, decides to follow him to the Celestial City, taking along her family: Matthew, James, Samuel, and Joseph. The latter, though referred to as "the children," must have been adolescents, for all get married along the way.

Mercy

A "comely" young woman, a friend and neighbor, who joins Christiana on her pilgrimage; later, marries Matthew.

Great-heart

A stalwart and well-armed Christian soldier, who is assigned by Interpreter to escort Christiana and her party to the Celestial Gate; he is a great giant-killer, and fond of giving religious advice and delivering sermonettes on almost any occasion.

Old Honest

Though a native of the Town of Stupidity, he has seen the "Light" and joins Christiana's party; while argumentative and long-winded, he is one of Bunyan's more engaging characters.

Gaius

"A very honorable disciple," who keeps a pleasant inn between the Valley of the Shadow of Death and Vanity Fair; it is he who, much to her surprise, tells Christiana of her husband's illustrious ancestry, going back to St. Peter, St. Paul, and other notables.

Mnason

A native of the island of Cyprus, at whose house the Pilgrims stay while at Vanity Fair; his daughters Grace and Martha are married to Christiana's unwedded sons, Samuel and Joseph.

Feeble-mind

A man of a "whitely look" who joins the Pilgrim party after being rescued from the hands of the giant Slay-good by Great-heart.

Ready-to-halt

A badly crippled man who also joins the pilgrimage even though he has to hobble along painfully on crutches.

Mr. Despondency and his daughter **Much-afraid**

Rescued from the dungeon in Doubting Castle when Great-heart leads an expedition to kill Giant Despair and tear down his castle; Despondency and Much-afraid join the pilgrimage and go on complaining to the end.

Valiant-for-truth

Another Christian sword-bearer and great giant-killer who carries and mightily wields "a right Jerusalem blade"; talks a lot, too.

Stand-fast

Who is met in the Enchanted Ground, kneeling on the path and imploring God for Christ's sake to save him from a "witch" who is determined to seduce him.

Madam Bubble

"A tall comely dame," carrying a huge purse filled with gold; she is the witch, "a bold and impudent slut," who tries to divert Stand-fast from his pious duty by offering him "her body, her purse, and her bed"; as he is poor and very sleepy at the moment, Stand-fast is sorely tempted to embrace her.

Assorted Giants, Fiends, Monsters, etc.

Grim, or Bloody-man, who emerges from a cave near Palace Beautiful and is beheaded by Great-heart; this giant symbolizes the civil authorities charged with enforcing the penal laws against Nonconformists.

Giant **Slay-good,** slain by Great-heart because he is a general nuisance around Gaius' inn and also a cannibal.

Maul, a giant who "spoils young Pilgrims with sophistry" (a symbol of the Roman Catholic Church); Great-heart stops all this by taking off the giant's head after a three-round fight.

An unnamed **beast** like "nothing ever seen before," a huge dragon with seven heads and ten horns (another symbol of the Roman Catholic Church); Great-heart fails to kill him, but inflicts such injuries that everyone is certain the monster will die of his wounds.

Giant **Despair,** who is done in by Great-heart and his friends in revenge for the indignities and cruelties heaped upon Christian, Hopeful, and other Pilgrims.

SUMMARIES AND COMMENTARIES

Part II of this book, like Part I, is a long continuous narrative, with no divisions, and the story accordingly will be dealt with in sections.

SECTION 1

To Palace Beautiful

Summary

Christian's wife, whom Bunyan names Christiana, misses her husband and begins to regret her refusal to go with him when he set out on his pilgrimage. She hears reports that Christian is faring very well in Heaven, having "already a very rich and pleasant dwelling at court," is eating and drinking well, sitting on the right hand of the Lord, from whom he receives many smiles and favors. It would be nice to be enjoying some of this, too. In addition, Christiana has become worried about the salvation of her soul and the salvation of her four children, all boys.

Should she now set out to trace her husband's footsteps in the hope of joining him in the raptures of the Celestial City? Sagacity and other of her friends encourage her to do so. Still others advise against it. Christiana cannot make up her mind until she is visited by an emissary who comes from Heaven to deliver to her a note from God, written "in letters of gold," and "it smelt after the manner of the best perfume" (Song of Sol. 1:3). The gist of the note is: "That the King would have her do as did Christian her husband, for that was the way to come to his City, and to dwell in his Presence with joy forever."

Gathering her children, who "burst out into tears for joy" at her decision, Christiana is packing up when two friends come in, Mrs. Timorous and Neighbor Mercy, both in great excitement. Mrs. Timorous is horrified that Christiana is going to sacrifice her "four sweet babes" in such a hazardous venture. But Neighbor Mercy finds that "her bowels yearned over Christiana," and even more "over her own soul (for what Christiana had said had taken some hold upon her mind)." She therefore says that she will accompany Christiana a little way on her journey. Meantime, Mrs. Timorous has run home and called in her favorite gossips—Mrs. Bat's-eyes, Mrs. Inconsiderate, Mrs. Light-mind, and Mrs. Know-nothing—who all agree that Christiana is a "blind and foolish woman."

Having walked a little way, Mercy decides that she will not turn back but go on with Christiana and the children. They pass without much difficulty through the Slough of Despond, in which Christian had floundered so badly, and come to the Wicket Gate, where Christiana knocks and is admitted with her children. Mercy is left outside and fearing that she has been rejected, falls in a faint. On Christiana's plea in her behalf, the gatekeeper comes out, takes Mercy by the hand, leads her inside, gives her some myrrh as smelling salts, and invites all in the party to rest themselves in a summer parlor. The Lord soon appears there to assure Mercy that she is welcome as a Pilgrim.

Proceeding, they have gone only a bow-shot or two from the Wicket Gate when they see two "very ill-favored ones" coming toward them. Christiana and Mercy drop their veils over their faces and attempt to pass by, but the men stop them, then try to embrace them. "Stand back," cries Christiana angrily, "and be gone, for we have no money to lose, being Pilgrims as you see...."

"We make no assault upon you for money," says one of the men, "but are come out to tell you that if you will but grant one small request. ...we will make women of you forever....We intend no hurt to your lives. 'Tis another thing we would have."

Christiana replies that she knows very well what they would have, but would rather die than give it. With that, she and Mercy let out a cry of "Murder, murder! and so put themselves under those laws that are provided for the protection of women" (Deut. 22:25-27). Their cries are heard at the Wicket Gate, and a figure named Reliever comes running to the rescue, arriving just in time to save Christiana and Mercy, finding each of them "in a very great scuffle," with the children standing by and wailing, not understanding what is going on.

Reliever chases away the "ruffians" (fiends) and then remarks his wonder why the two "weak" women, when at the Wicket Gate, had not petitioned the Lord "for a conductor." Because, says Christiana, "who could have thought that so near the King's palace there should have lurked such naughty ones?" Indeed, it would have been better to have asked for a conductor, Christiana grants, "but since our Lord knew 'twould be for our profit, I wonder he sent not one along with us!" Reliever explains that it is often better not to grant things not asked for, because things unasked for are usually held in "little esteem." One should ask of God and, if circumstances warrant, it will be given.

The next stop is at Interpreter's House, where the party is warmly welcomed after Christiana has introduced herself as the wife of Christian, whom Interpreter well remembers from his visit some years before. Interpreter shows Christiana and Mercy what he had shown to Christian—the man in the iron cage, the man awakening from a bad dream, and other "excellent things"—but also something more. Interpreter leads them into a room where there is a man who can "look no way but downwards, with a muck-rake in his hand." Above him stands one holding a Celestial crown, offering it to Muck-rake, but the latter does not look up and goes on raking "to himself the straws, the small sticks, and dust on the floor."

"I know somewhat the meaning of this," says Christiana, "for this is a figure of a man of this world, is it not, good sir?" Yes it is, says Interpreter, who then has a damsel named Innocent lead them into the garden of the bath, "wash them, and make them clean," for so the Lord would have women who come into his presence. Emerging from the bath, Christiana and Mercy are "not only sweet and clean, but also much enlivened and strengthened in their joints." Interpreter then asks Innocent to go into the vestry and bring out new raiment, "fine linen, white and clean," and summoning his man servant Great-heart, orders him to take up sword, shield, and helmet, and escort "these my daughters...to the house called Beautiful, at which place they will rest next."

Coming to the base of Difficulty Hill, Great-heart shows Christiana and Mercy the bypaths by which Formalist and Hypocrisy, traveling with Christian, had hoped to get around the hill and had perished, which prompts Christiana to remark: "The way of transgressors is hard" (Prov. 13:15). Climbing the steep hill, all begin to pant; Mercy wants to sit down; the youngest child begins to cry. Picking up the child, Great-heart urges them to keep going until they reach the Prince's arbor halfway up the "breathing hill."

Here they are all happy to sit down and rest as Christian had done. Christiana brings out a bit to eat, given to her by Interpreter—"a piece of pomegranate...also a piece of honeycomb and a little bottle of spirits." Having rested and refreshed themselves, they start climbing again but soon stop when Christiana discovers that she has forgotten her bottle of spirits and sends one of her boys back to fetch it. "I think this is a losing place," says Mercy. "Here Christian lost his Roll, and here Christiana left her bottle behind her. Sir, what is the cause of this?" Great-heart replies that the cause is sleep and forgetfulness: "Some sleep when they should keep awake; and some forget when they should remember."

Satisfied with this explanation of the obvious, they go on till they catch sight of the lions in front of the gate to Palace Beautiful. As Great-heart advances with drawn sword, he is confronted by a giant named Grim, or Bloody-man, who suddenly emerges from a cave and bellows that no one is to pass. After some argument Great-heart rushes at him, knocks him to his knees, breaks his helmet, cuts off an arm, and leaves him sprawling, dead, on the ground. He then leads the trembling women and boys past the lions and up the lane to the gatehouse of the palace.

That accomplished, Great-heart announces he is returning to Interpreter's House that night. Christiana, Mercy, and the boys plead with him to stay and escort them the rest of the way. Great-heart explains that he cannot because of his orders from the Lord. But he adds, consolingly, that if he were again assigned to escort them, he would willingly do so.

Commentary

In Part I, as will be recalled, Bunyan "dreamed" his tale of Christian and his pilgrimage while lying in jail, locked up for his nonconformist practices and beliefs proscribed by law. In Part II, he dreams of the adventures of Christiana and her children while sleeping in a wood, which he places about a mile from the City of Destruction.

The first figure to be introduced is an old gentleman, Mr. Sagacity, who relates to the dreamer how well Christian is faring up above and the news that his wife Christiana has decided to take the children and follow him to the Celestial City after receiving from God a personal note urging her to do as Christian did and thus share with him the countless joys of eternal life on Mount Zion. Christiana and her children, and her friend Mercy, do not appear and speak in person till they are already on their journey and past the Slough of Despond.

The use of Sagacity as the first character is an ingenious and effective story-telling device. It enables Bunyan to set the base and the background of the story not in straightaway narrative exposition, which could be very dull, but rather in the far more interesting form of an enlightening conversation between Sagacity and the dreamer. In telling any story, dialogue is always more effective than mere exposition.

Though it is not explicitly stated, Christiana's friend and companion, the warm-hearted and "comely" Mercy, is an unmarried maiden, evidently in her late teens, for on the pilgrimage she becomes the bride of one of the "children," Matthew, Christiana's oldest son.

It is significant that Christiana and her party have little trouble in overcoming the first obstacle, the Slough of Despond, in which Christian, weighed down by doubts and fears, and by the heavy sack of sins on his shoulders, had so floundered and almost been "smothered with mud." As soon as the party is safely across, Christiana hears a voice saying: "Blessed is she that believeth, for there shall be a performance of the things that have been told her from the Lord."

In this second part of the book, Bunyan expands on his description of the Wicket Gate, the entrance to the Holy Way. Christian's reception here was quite simple. After knocking a time or two, Christian had been admitted by the gatekeeper, Good-will, who talked with him a bit before sending him on toward Interpreter's House. But when Christiana knocks, a great dog, a huge mastiff, comes bounding out, barking ferociously. Afraid of being torn to pieces, the women and children draw back, not knowing what to do. Summoning her courage, Christiana knocks again. The gatekeeper calls the dog off and after Christiana has identified herself and her "sweet babes," invites them to come in and shuts the gate, at the same time ordering "a trumpeter...to entertain Christiana with shouting and sound of trumpet for joy" [Luke 15:7]. The air resounds with "melodious notes."

Christiana, though grateful, rather sharply asks the gatekeeper why he keeps such a dog in his yard. The "filthy cur," it appears, does not belong to him, but to Satan, who uses it to scare Pilgrims away from the Holy Way. "But I take all at present patiently," the gatekeeper explains. "I also give my Pilgrims timely help, so they are not delivered up to his power, to do to them what his doggish nature would prompt him to do." Besides, the dog has often frightened Pilgrims enough to make them move "from worse to better."

Left outside the gate, thinking herself abandoned, Mercy swoons. But on Christiana's plea in her behalf, she is helped to her feet by the gatekeeper and taken inside, and all the weary Pilgrims are escorted to a pleasant "summer parlor," where they rest themselves for a time. Mercy continues to be worried about her status. Christiana is carrying a personal invitation from the Lord to come to Heaven, while Mercy has only the sponsorship of Christiana. To allay her anxieties, the Lord soon appears to assure Mercy that she can go on confidently toward the Celestial City.

The scene just beyond the Wicket Gate where two "very ill-favored" men accost Christiana and Mercy and attempt first to seduce them and then to rape them is the only scene of its kind in the entire book—one of the few with a slightly erotic flavor.

At Interpreter's House, Bunyan also adds new details. Christiana's party is shown all the things seen by Christian: the portrait of Evangelist, the man in the iron cage, and the man trembling violently as he awakens from a bad dream in which he sees himself called to Judgment when he is not ready for it. In addition to these and other "excellent things," the women and children are led into a large room where there is a man with a "muck-rake" in his hand. Over his head appears a figure offering him a "Celestial crown." But the man does not look up, only down, and goes on raking "the straws, the small sticks, and dust on the floor." Primarily, "muck" means barnyard manure, filth, anything disgusting, and not such trivia as straws, twigs, and dust.

Having specific reference to this passage, the word "muckraker" has come into the English—or at least the American—language as a term of criticism, reproach, and even of abuse. The epithet became popular after 1906 when President Theodore Roosevelt used it to characterize and stigmatize an influential group of authors and journalists who were seriously concerned about the iniquities and the inequities in American life, and were brilliantly exposing the roots of the trouble, finding them in the widespread corruption in politics and business.

SECTION 2

Palace Beautiful

Summary

Having led Christiana and her party up the lane to Palace Beautiful over the dead body of Grim and in despite of the lions, Great-heart departs to return to Interpreter's House, his assignment fulfilled. Explaining who she is to a virgin of the Palace, a damsel named Humble-mind, Christiana and her party are invited in and led to a very large room where they are greeted, each with a kiss, by the members of the family, who join in saying: "Welcome, ye vessels of the Grace of God; welcome to us, your friends."

Though the Pilgrims are very tired and anxious for rest and sleep, they are persuaded to refresh themselves "with a morsel of meat [Exod. 12: 3, 8] for they had prepared for them a lamb [John 1:29], with the accustomed sauce belonging thereto." When Christiana asks if they may sleep in the room where her husband slept, her request is granted. As they are falling asleep, they hear "a noise of music," and Mercy exclaims: "Wonderful! Music in the house, music in the heart, and music also in Heaven, for joy that we are here."

In the morning, the Pilgrims are invited to stay at the palace as long as they like, and they accept, staying a month or more, which gives the maidens many opportunities to catechize the children on their knowledge of things divine and give them some needed lessons.

While at the palace, Mercy has something of a romance. Being "of fair countenance, and therefore the more alluring," she catches the eye of a Mr. Brisk, "a man of some breeding, and one that pretended to religion." When he comes to call, he finds Mercy always busy making garments, hose, and other things. Her industry impresses Mr. Brisk, who decides that Mercy, in addition to her charms, would make him a good and useful wife. After several visits, Mr. Brisk asks how much she earns a day from her work. "I do these things," Mercy explains, "that I may be rich in good works, laying up in store a good foundation against the time to come, that I may lay hold on Eternal Life." Yes, says Mr. Brisk, but just exactly what does she do with the things she makes?

Shocked when told that she gives them away to clothe the naked, he comes no more a-courting, explaining that Mercy is "a pretty lass, but troubled with ill conditions" (i.e., characteristics, habits of mind). Hearing of this, Mercy remarks that she might have had husbands before, but they were such as Mr. Brisk who "did not like my conditions, though never did any of them find fault with my person.... Well, if nobody will have me, I will die a maid, or my conditions shall be to me as a husband, for I cannot change my nature." Prudence, one of the palace virgins, observes that Mercy has become little more than a name, and that practice of it is anathema to all but a few.

One of Christiana's boys becomes very sick—the oldest son, Matthew (for the first time, the boys are given names). The virgins summon "one Mr. Skill, an ancient and well-approved physician," who diagnoses the complaint as "the gripes" and asks Christiana what the boy has been eating of late. Nothing but the most wholesome food, Christiana replies. But Mr. Skill is skeptical, saying: "This boy has been tampering with something that lies in his maw undigested.... he must be purged, or else he will die."

One of the younger sons, Samuel, speaks up: "Mother, what was that which my brother did gather up and eat so soon as we were come from the [Wicket] gate?... You know there was an orchard on the left hand, on the other side of the wall, and some of the trees hung over the wall, and my brother did plash [knock down the fruit] and did eat."

It was as he thought, Mr. Skill observes, and the fruit eaten by Matthew was the worst of all: "It is the fruit of Beelzebub's orchard. I do marvel that none did warn you of it; many have died thereof." Christiana begins to weep and cries out: "O naughty boy, and O careless mother." The doctor comforts her by telling her to be not too much dejected, for he would mix a concoction to make the boy "purge and vomit."

His first concoction is "made of the blood of a goat, the ashes of a heifer, and with some of the juice of hyssop, etc" [Heb. 10:1-4]. When this concoction proves to be too weak, Mr. Skill mixes another, "*Ex carne et sanguine Christi*" [John 6:53-58]. Here Bunyan adds, "(You know physicians give strange medicines to their patients.)" The second stronger concoction is made up into pills, "with a promise or two, and a proportionate quantity of salt" [Mark 9:49]. Three of these pills are to be taken "at a time, fasting, and half a quarter of a pint of the tears of repentance" [Heb. 9:14; Zach. 12:10]. Though he resists at first, Matthew finally swallows this medicine, which "wrought kindly with him. It caused him to purge, it caused him to sleep and rest quietly, it put him into a fine heat and breathing sweat, and did quite rid him of his gripes."

Quite impressed, Christiana asks Mr. Skill what else his pill is good for. "It is a universal pill," the doctor replies, a sure cure for everything, and if properly prepared, remains effective forever. Christiana asks the doctor to make up for her twelve boxes of the stuff, swearing that she and her family will never use any other physic.

During his stay at Palace Beautiful, Christian had been shown many of the "rarities" of the place, including, as will be remembered, a birth certificate attesting that the Lord was "the son of the Ancient of Days," begotten by "eternal generation." Christiana and those with her are shown things even more remarkable: "one of the apples that Eve did eat of," as did Adam, for which "both were turned out of Paradise"; Jacob's Ladder, up which some angels are clambering to Heaven; a Golden Anchor, which is presented to Christiana to help her "stand steadfast" in stormy weather; and "the mount upon which Abraham our father offered up Isaac his son," and where there is still to be seen "the altar, the wood, the fire, and the knife" used on that occasion.

"Oh, what a man... was Abraham!" they exclaim, and bless themselves. After this, Prudence leads them back to the palace and into the dining room, where she begins to play on a "pair of excellent virginals."

Preparing to end their long stay with the virgins, Christiana sends a note to Interpreter, petitioning him to send back Great-heart to escort her and her weak Pilgrim band on the rest of their journey—a request that is granted. As soon as Great-heart appears, they are on their way again, descending a steep, slippery slope into the Valley of Humiliation.

Commentary

As symbols of the church and church fellowship, Bunyan here expatiates at length, as he did in Part I, on the amenities of Palace Beautiful and the virtues of the maidens there. In this book, as in his other writings, Bunyan stresses time and again the important work and functions performed by women in the church. They represent its gentler side, in contrast to the men who, it is suggested, should all be sword-carrying Christian soldiers, ready to hack down giants, monsters, and all forms of corporeal evil in their way.

The first supper offered to Christiana and her party at Palace Beautiful, where the virgins prepared for them "a lamb [John 1:29], with the accustomed sauce [wine] belonging thereto," symbolizes the admission of new members to the Church and the partaking together of Holy Communion (body of the "lamb"). It should be noted that Bunyan did not regard church membership as indispensable for salvation, but always highly praised it as opening an excellent way to Mount Zion.

In giving Mercy's suitor the name of Mr. Brisk, Bunyan was using the term in an older and now obsolete sense, signifying someone who is pert, objectionably smart, exuding self-confidence, a good entrepreneur. Mr. Brisk loses interest in Mercy when he finds out that she does not sell the clothes she makes for money, but gives them away. What kind of housewife would she make! After Mercy has been jilted by Mr. Brisk, her marriage not long after to Matthew, Christian's oldest son, comes as something of an anticlimax.

In Part I, Bunyan described Ignorance as a "very brisk lad" from the country of Conceit. This was unfair. He was no more preoccupied with his own conceits than Christian was. He was "ignorant" only in that he did not think that Christian (Bunyan's alter ego) knew everything about everything. There were other points of view, and Ignorance stoutly defended his.

While at Palace Beautiful, when Matthew falls sick from eating fruit gathered along the Holy Way and Christiana requests a doctor, Mr. Skill, the latter diagnoses the illness as very serious, one of which many have died. Matthew had eaten forbidden fruit, out of Satan's orchard. The forbidden fruit represents original sin, and Dr. Skill cures it by concocting a "universal pill....good against all the diseases that Pilgrims are incident to." It is made *Ex carne et sanguine Christi* (from the body and blood of Christ). Here, in what he calls his borrowed Latin, Bunyan is imitating the jargon used in medical presciptions of the day, many being much like Mr. Skill's first but too weak concoction made of the blood of a goat, the ashes of a heifer, etc. There is much interesting misinformation in the pharmacopoeias of the day.

After Matthew has been cured of the "gripes" and vows not to eat "any more green plums," he approaches Prudence, one of the virgins, and begins to question her about various things; an interesting colloquy ensues:

Why is physic so bitter to the taste? "To show how unwelcome the Word of God and the effects thereof are to a carnal heart."

But why, in doing good, does physic cause one to purge and vomit? "To show that the Word, when it works effectually, cleanseth the heart and mind."

Why do the flames of a fire go upward, and the beams of the sun downward? "By the going up of the fire we are taught to ascend to Heaven by fervent and hot desires. And by the sun sending his heat, beams...downwards, we are taught that the Saviour of the world, though high, reaches down his Grace and love to us below."

Where do clouds get their water? "Out of the sea." And what is the lesson of that? "That ministers should fetch their doctrine from God."

Why is the rainbow caused by the sun? "To show that the covenant of God's Grace is confirmed to us in Christ."

Why do springs from the sea come to us through the earth? "To show that the Grace of God comes to us through the body of Christ." Why are some springs in high places? "To show that the spirit of Grace shall spring up in some that are great and mighty, as well as in many that are poor and low."

Why does fire cling to the candle wick? "To show that unless Grace doth kindle upon the heart, there will be no true light of life in us."

Why does the pelican pierce her breast with her bill? (an old superstition). "To nourish her young ones with her blood, and thereby show that Christ, the blessed, so loveth his young as to save them from death by his Blood."

And what may be learned from hearing a cock crow? "Learn to remember Peter's sin and Peter's repentance. The cock's crowing shows also that day is coming on. Let then the crowing of the cock put thee in mind of that last and terrible Day of Judgment."

This is a wholly mystical explanation of natural phenomena, worlds apart from the disciplines and concepts of science.

SECTION 3

Valley of Humiliation and Gaius' Inn

Summary

Descending from Palace Beautiful into the Valley of Humiliation, Christiana becomes very apprehensive, recalling that it was here that Christian had encountered and been almost killed by that "foul fiend," Apollyon. She is reassured by Great-heart, who says that "here is nothing to hurt us unless we procure it to ourselves." The valley turns out to be as Great-heart said it would be, "as fruitful a place as any the crow flies over."

It now appears that Christian had brought Apollyon upon himself, as it were, because of his slips and derelictions along the Holy Way. He had been too proud, too self-satisfied, and needed a bit of humiliation, which was arranged by the Lord, or rather, by Satan, always willing to oblige in punishing sinners. Mercy, for her part, finds the green and solitary Valley of Humiliation the pleasantest spot she has ever seen: "I love to be in such places where there is no rattling with coaches, nor rumbling with wheels. Methinks here one may without molestation be thinking what he is, whence he came, what he has done, and what the King has called him. Here one may think, and break at heart, and melt in one's spirit, until one's eyes become like the fishpools of Heshbon" (Song of Sol. 7:4).

Passing by a monument erected to commemorate Christian's victory over Apollyon, Great-heart leads his charges into the Valley of the Shadow of Death, where they hear "a groaning as of dead men.... words of lamentation as if spoken by some in extreme Torment....a kind of hissing as of serpents," and then, the ground under their feet begins to shake. Out of fright, one of the children gets sick, but Christiana revives him by giving him three of Mr. Skill's magic pills and some of the spirits presented to her by Interpreter.

As the party moves on, Christiana sees something in the road ahead of them, and all are frightened. Great-heart tells them to keep close to him and lets the Fiend approach. When the latter sees that Great-heart is prepared to do battle, he vanishes into thin air, which reminds Christiana of the old saying, "Resist the Devil, and he will fly from you." Great-heart also scares away a lion that comes up behind them, roaring so loudly that the whole valley echoes.

Having passed through a place "of great stinks and loathsome smells," they meet "Maul, a giant," who emerges from a cave to challenge Great-heart, charging him with being a kidnaper who gathers up women and children, carrying "them into a strange country, to the weakening of my master's kingdom." It is his duty to lead sinners from darkness to light, replies Great-heart, "and if this be indeed the ground of thy quarrel, let us fall to it as soon as thou wilt." Great-heart draws his sword, Maul picks up his huge club, and with his first blow knocks Great-heart to his knees. Staggering up, the latter pinks the giant in the arm. After an hour of swinging and sweating, the combatants sit down for a rest, as the women and children stand by sighing and crying.

The battle is soon resumed, being fought somewhat like a modern boxing match. Round One was a draw. In Round Two, having been knocked down with a full blow, the giant asks Great-heart to hold up and allow him to recover. "So Mr. Great-heart fairly lets him get up." Round Two is clearly Great-heart's. After another rest, they go at it again. At the start of Round Three, Maul brings his big club down heavily on Great-heart's head and all but cracks his skull. Now thoroughly aroused, Great-heart charges his adversary "in the full heat of his spirit, and pierceth him under the fifth rib." As the giant begins to faint, Great-heart follows up his blow, and severs "the head of the giant from his shoulders." The women and children rejoice, Great-heart offers praise to God for his deliverance, and they all sit down to "eat and drink and make merry."

A little farther on, they come to an oak under which is sleeping an old man, whom they recognize as a Pilgrim "by his clothes and his staff and his girdle." Being awakened, he identifies himself as Old Honest. Though from the Town of Stupidity, he has seen the Light, he says, and is now on his way to the Celestial City. After a long conversation about the renown of Christian, the trials of a Mr. Fearing, who "stumbled at every straw," and the vices of Mr. Self-will, Christiana asks Old Honest if he knows of an inn where she and the children may rest themselves, for they are very weary.

Honest guides them to a tavern kept by a "very honorable disciple, one Gaius," who has rooms for all of them and goes to tell the cook, Taste-that-which-is-good (not one of Bunyan's happier inspirations in coining names), to prepare a good supper. A cloth is spread on the table and after trenchers, salt, and bread have been brought in, supper is served, and it is a feast of many courses:

First, "a heave-shoulder and a wave-breast . . . to show that they must begin their meal with prayer and praise to God" (Lev. 7:32-34; 10:14-15; Ps. 25:1; Heb. 13:15); then a bottle of wine, "red as blood. . . . the juice of the true vine that makes glad the heart of God and man. So they drank and were merry" (Deut. 32:14, Judg. 9:13; John 15:1); next a "dish of milk, well crumbed," for the boys, and a "dish of butter and honey," good for cheering people's hearts and strengthening their judgment and understanding, "our Lord's dish when he was a child"; all of this topped off with apples and a "dish of nuts" (Song of Sol. 6:11). Some at the table remark that nuts spoil tender teeth, especially the teeth of children. This inspires Gaius to reply in verse:

> Hard texts are nuts (I will not call them cheaters),
> Whose shells do keep their kernels from the eaters.
> Ope then the shells, and you shall have the meat;
> They here are brought for you to crack and eat.

So they sit at the table "very merry," talking and drinking, cracking nuts and cracking riddles, having such a good time that all but the boys stay up all night. Gaius' Inn is altogether such a pleasant place that Christiana and her party, on being invited, stay more than a month.

During their stay, Gaius informs Christiana to her surprise that her husband, whom she had known as a poor, ragged man, came of most distinguished stock. His ancestors, who "dwelt first at Antioch" (Acts 11:26), included many an ancient saint, prophet, and martyr: Paul and Peter, and Stephen, who "was knocked on the head with stones"; Romanus, "whose flesh was cut in pieces from his bones"; Ignatius, "who was cast to the lions"; Marcus of Arethusa, who "was hanged up in a basket in the sun for the wasps to eat." In view of this, Christian's name and character should never be forgotten. His line should be perpetuated, Gaius insists, suggesting to Christiana that Mercy should be induced to marry her oldest son, Matthew, this being "the way to preserve you a posterity on the earth." Mercy is not averse, and Matthew takes her to wife. Then Gaius gives his daughter Phoebe in marriage to another of Christian's sons, young James.

Though delighted with all this, Great-heart is restless, wishing to exercise his sword a bit, asking Gaius if there is not something he could be doing to clean up the neighborhood. Yes indeed, says Gaius, there is a giant named Slay-good, who much annoys Pilgrims along this stretch of the King's highway. Seeking out Slay-good, Great-heart finds him frisking the pockets of a captured Pilgrim named Feeble-mind, intending later "to pick his bones," for the giant is a flesh-eater. After a few preliminaries, Great-heart and Slay-good go at it in a fight that lasts about an hour. Vanquishing Slay-good, Great-heart cuts off the giant's head and returns with it to the inn, bringing along Feeble-mind.

A sickly man, the rescued Pilgrim is feeble both in mind and body, but not in spirit, for he is resolved to get to Heaven even if he has to crawl there. After telling his story, he is invited to join Christiana's party in accord with the will of the Lord "that comfort should be given to the feeble-minded" (1 Thess. 5:14).

Shortly, there is a knock at the inn door, and Gaius goes out to find there another Pilgrim, a man on crutches, Mr. Ready-to-halt. He, too, is invited to join Christiana's party, which here acquires four new members: Old Honest, Feeble-mind, Ready-to-halt, and Phoebe, James' bride.

The group is now so large that when it takes to the road again, making for the town of Vanity Fair, it has to walk in column along the narrow way—with Great-heart and Old Honest up front; Christiana and her four boys, Mercy, and Phoebe coming next; and poor Feeble-mind and Ready-to-halt hobbling along behind, doing their best to keep up.

Commentary

The Valley of Humiliation, as will be recalled, proved to be a terror to Christian. It was there he was almost overcome by the fiend Apollyon. Altogether, he found it to be a dark, gloomy, frightening place. It is both interesting and significant that Christiana and her party find it to be so very different. Mercy remarks that it is the pleasantest spot she has ever seen. It is "fat ground," with spreading green meadows "beautified with lilies" (Song of Sol. 2:1; James 4:6; 1 Pet. 5:5), filled with quietly grazing flocks of sheep. There is here no rattling of coaches, nor rumbling of wheels. "Methinks," says Mercy, "here one may without much molestation be thinking what he is, whence he came, what he has done, and to what the King has called him."

The Valley of Humiliation, it appears, is not really a place. It is a state of mind, a quality of heart and spirit. It reflects what one brings to it. Bunyan explains it this way in a song by a shepherd boy: "He that is down needs fear no fall" in the Valley of Humiliation. "He that is humble ever shall have God to be his guide." Christian had got into trouble here because he had been too proud of himself. His encounter with Apollyon was the "fruit of those slips" he had made along the way, such as his carelessness in falling asleep on Difficulty Hill and temporarily losing his precious Roll, his passport to Heaven. He should have laid more store by the Lord's favors.

Nor does Christiana's group have too much difficulty in traversing the Valley of the Shadow of Death, though they do meet a giant named Maul, who harms "young Pilgrims with sophistry." The giant, a symbol of the Roman Catholic Church, charges the Pilgrims with being kidnapers. They gather up women and children and carry them "into a strange country," to the weakening of the power of the pope. The Roman Church had long vehemently and often violently opposed Protestant proselytizing. It comes as no surprise to the reader that, in the battle between the two, Great-heart knocks Maul down and takes off his head. To represent that Great-heart's triumph meant the overthrow and end of the Roman Church was merely wishful thinking on Bunyan's part.

The scene at Gaius' Inn has several interesting aspects. A newcomer among the Pilgrims, long-winded and argumentative Old Honest from the Town of Stupidity, is one of Bunyan's more engaging characters. In one argument, Great-heart has to take him down a bit, telling him "not to be so hot," that he is among friends, and stop shouting. Another Pilgrim appears, a man on crutches, Mr. Ready-to-halt, who is determined to get to the Celestial City even if he has to go on hands and knees. He is admitted into the inn and into the company of Christiana and her group. All give the crippled man very special attention.

The supper laid by Gaius on the day of the Pilgrims' arrival is a rather sumptuous one, with many courses and plenty of wine, "red as blood." The first course consists of a "heave-shoulder and a wave-breast." These refer to the right shoulder and a slice of the breast cut from an animal that a priest is about to offer as a sacrifice to God. The specific reference is to Lev. 7:32, 34; 10:14: "And the right shoulder shall ye give unto the priest for an heave offering of the sacrifices of your peace offerings....For the wave breast and the heave shoulder have I taken of the children of Israel from off the sacrifices of their peace offerings....And the wave breast and the heave shoulder shall ye eat in a clean place."

The lavish supper ends with the company cracking nuts and cracking riddles, for hard texts are nuts, says Gaius, "brought for you to crack and eat." The riddles, all of them along theological lines, are pretty feeble. Great-heart propounds this to Old Honest:

> He that will kill, must first to overcome;
> Who live abroad would, first must die at home.

Saying that this is a very hard one to crack, Mr. Honest tries to turn it over to Gaius, who refuses to become involved, saying that the question was not addressed to him. After some thought, Old Honest comes up with an answer, perhaps as good and clear as could be expected:

> He first by Grace must conquered be,
> That sin would mortify;
> And who, that lives, would convince me,
> Unto himself must die.

When Gaius informs Christiana, much to her surprise, of her husband's illustrious forebears—St. Peter, St. Paul, St. James, St. Stephen, among others—he remarks that Christian's ancestors "dwelt first at Antioch." This refers to Acts 11:26, which reads: "And the disciples were called Christians first in Antioch," an ancient city in Asia Minor, in what is now Turkey. Paul, Peter, and Barnabas had evangelized there.

SECTION 4

Vanity Fair and Doubting Castle

Summary

Proceeding from Gaius' Inn to the outskirts of Vanity Fair, the Pilgrim party halts there to consider the best way of passing through the town where Christian and Faithful had been given such a rough time—Faithful, after a trial before Lord Hate-good, having been mercilessly beaten and then burned at the stake. Saying that he knows a place where they might perhaps find lodgings, at the house of "one Mr. Mnason, a Cyprusian [a native of the island of Cyprus],...an old disciple," Great-heart leads them there. As it is dark, they are not seen as they enter the town and make their way to Mnason's house, where they are welcomed.

Old Honest asks his host if there are any good people in town. A few, Mnason replies. How might one meet them, Honest then inquires, "for the sight of good men to them that are going on pilgrimage is like to the appearing of the moon and the stars to them that are sailing upon the seas." Mnason stamps his foot, his daughter Grace appears, and she is dispatched to invite some of his friends to come over for the evening—Mr. Contrite, Mr. Holy-man, Mr. Love-saint, Mr. Dare-not-lie, and Mr. Penitent. In course of the conversation the Pilgrims learn that the people of the town are now more moderate than they were, having been much impressed by the fortitude Christian and Faithful displayed in their trials here. Indeed, since the scourging and burning of Faithful, "they have been ashamed to burn any more." Good people can now walk the streets unafraid.

The Pilgrims stay in Vanity Fair for some time, getting acquainted with the good people in the town, doing them many services. Great-heart here does battle with a monster "like unto no one beast upon the earth," having a body "like a dragon, and... seven heads and ten horns." As this monster is carrying off children from the town and wreaking great havoc generally, he has to be disposed of. With some townsmen, Great-heart goes after the beast not once, but many times, and though he does not succeed in slaying him and taking off his seven heads as a trophy, he makes him lame and so severely cuts him up that it seems certain the monster will soon die of his wounds.

During the long stay at the Fair, there is romance and joyous celebration of more marriages. Mnason gives daughters to the two unmarried sons among Christian's "children" – Grace to Samuel, Martha to Joseph. It is noted that all of the brides, Mercy, Phoebe, and the two recent ones, are "very fruitful, so that Christian's name, as was said before, was like to live in world."

Taking to the road again, the Pilgrim company comes to the River of God, or the River of the Water of Life, its banks lined with fine trees and meadows that remain green the year round. Here, by the riverside, are sheepfolds and a house, kept by Compassion and "built for the nourishing and bringing up of those lambs, the babes of those women that go on pilgrimage." Christiana admonishes her four daughters-in-law to commit their "little ones" to the care of Compassion, "so that, by these waters, they might be housed, harbored, succoured, and nourished, and that none of them might be lacking in time to come."

Going on, the party reaches By-path Meadow, into which Christian and Hopeful had erred and been captured by Giant Despair, almost losing their lives in his Doubting Castle dungeon. After some discussion, it is decided that an attempt should be made to slay Giant Despair, tear down his castle, and rescue any Pilgrims in his dungeon. Advancing with Old Honest and Christiana's four sons, Great-heart knocks on the castle gate with a terrific banging. Who is making all that racket? the giant wants to know. "It is I, Great-heart, one of the King of the Celestial Country's conductors of Pilgrims to their place.... open thy gates for my entrance. Prepare thyself also to fight."

The giant, having conquered angels, has no fears. Smiling at the vain effrontery of the challengers at the gate, he puts on his armor and comes out, a steel cap on his head, a breastplate of fire, wearing iron shoes, and grasping a huge club in his hand. The six men go at him from all sides. When the giant's wife Diffidence comes to his aid, Old Honest cuts her down with one stroke. With all fighting for their lives, Giant Despair is finally knocked to the ground and though he struggles hard, having "as many lives as a cat," is dispatched by Great-heart, who cuts off his head to add to his trophies.

The Pilgrim party then proceeds to tear down Doubting Castle, which takes a week. In the dungeon, filled with dead men's bones, they find and rescue two Pilgrims, Mr. Despondency and his daughter Much-afraid, whom they take back with them to the Holy Way, together with the head of the giant, which is posted on a pole by the lane as a warning not to molest Pilgrims.

At sight of the bloody head, Feeble-mind and Ready-to-halt become "jocund and merry," and music is called for. It now appears, though not mentioned before, that Christiana has been carrying along a viol, and Mercy a lute. They strike up a tune, which inspires in Ready-to-halt a desire to dance. Taking Miss Much-afraid by the hand, he performs sprightfully, even though on crutches, and so the Pilgrims go merrily on their way toward the Celestial Mountains.

Commentary

In picturing the people of Vanity Fair as being more moderate than they had been at the time of Christian's visit, Bunyan was alluding to the fact that prosecutions and persecutions of Nonconformists had slackened since the passage in 1672 of the Declaration of Indulgence, to which Bunyan owed his release from his first imprisonment, which had stretched out for twelve years. Such prosecutions and persecutions would begin again and become increasingly sharp until James II, an avowed Papist, was dethroned in the Glorious Revolution of 1688, the year of Bunyan's death.

The scene at the house of the Pilgrims' host, Mr. Mnason, is a pleasant one. During the Pilgrims' stay there of a month or more, Great-heart continues his hunt for giants and fiends in general. In the woods outside Vanity Fair, there lurks a "monster" which sallies forth now and again to slaughter people in the town. This monster, a dragon with seven heads and ten horns, is another symbol of the Roman Church. Great-heart moves against him but cannot slay him, being disappointed in not succeeding as he had with the giant Maul, also a symbol of the Roman Church. But Great-heart succeeds in laming the monster, and "it is verily believed by some that this beast will die of his wound." Here, again, Bunyan was indulging in some wishful thinking.

The women, children, and cripples in Christiana's party rejoice with song and dance when the Christian warriors, led by Great-heart, return in triumph from their assault on Doubting Castle, bringing back the head of Giant Despair, after having killed him and demolished his castle. They set the head on a pole beside the King's highway. So that no reader will miss the moral here, Bunyan places a marble slab by the pole, inscribed thus in very lame verse:

> This is the head of him, whose name only
> In former times did Pilgrims terrify.
> His castle's down, and Diffidence his wife

Brave Master Great-heart has bereft of life....
This head also, when doubting cripples dance,
Doth show from fears they have deliverance.

SECTION 5

Delectable Mountains and over the River

Summary

Arriving at the Delectable Mountains, Christiana and her party are welcomed by the shepherds as warmly as Christian and Hopeful had been. The shepherds show special concern about the weaker in the company—Mr. Feeble-mind, Mr. Ready-to-halt, Mr. Despondency and his daughter Much-afraid. These are singled out by name and invited to be the first to enter the palace on the mountains.

Next morning, the leading shepherds, Knowledge, Experience, Watchful, and Sincere, take the Pilgrims to see the sights, not only those shown to Christian, but others: Mount Marvel, from which they perceive in the distance a man who tumbles "the hills about with words....set there to teach Pilgrims how to believe down, or tumble out of their ways, what difficulties they shall meet with, by Faith" (Mark 11:23-24); Mount Innocent, where they see "a man clothed all in white" (Mr. Godly-man) and two men, Prejudice and Ill-will, continuously casting dirt on him, but the dirt does not stick and his raiment remains shining because of the "innocency of his life"; Mount Charity, where a man sits with a bundle of cloth before him, cutting out coats and garments for the poor, yet his bundle of cloth never grows less. "He that watereth shall be watered himself. And the cake that the widow gave to the Prophet did not cause that she had ever the less in her barrel."

Mercy, "being a young and breeding woman," sees something in the palace that she longs to have, but is ashamed to ask for it. It is a looking glass in the dining room. She has her mind so set on having it, she tells her mother-in-law Christiana, "that if I have it not, I think I shall miscarry." Perhaps the shepherds would be willing to sell it. Christiana says that she will see what can be done about it.

"Now the glass was one of a thousand. It would present a man one way, with his own features exactly, and turn it but another way and it would show one the very face and similitude of the Prince of Pilgrims himself....the very Crown of Thorns upon his head...the holes in his hands, in his feet, and his side." The shepherds are very pleased to present Mercy with the wonderful glass, and bestow gifts on Christiana and the other women – bracelets and necklaces, "earrings for their ears, and jewels on their foreheads."

When Christian and Hopeful were leaving the Delectable Mountains, the shepherds gave them written instructions on what to do and what to avoid on the rest of their journey. By forgetting to read these "cautions," Christian and Hopeful had stumbled into serious troubles. There is no need for the shepherds to give Christiana's party any cautions, for it is led by Great-heart, who, having frequently passed this way, knows all about it.

Proceeding, they soon come to a man standing in the road with his sword drawn and his face all bloody. When questioned, the man replies that his name is Valiant-for-truth, a Pilgrim from Dark-land, bound for the Celestial City, adding that he has just been attacked by three men, Wild-head, Inconsiderate, and Pragmatic, who tried to prevent his going forward. After a fierce three-hour battle, he had routed them. Asking to see his sword, Great-heart examines it and exclaims: "Ha, it is a right Jerusalem blade" (Isa. 2:3).

"It is so," Valiant-for-truth agrees. "Let a man have one of these blades, with a hand to wield it and skill to use it, and he may venture upon an angel with it....Its edges will never blunt. It will cut flesh and bones and soul and spirit and all" (Eph. 6:12-17; Heb. 4:12).

Valiant-for-truth joins the party and as they go along, relates his story. Great-heart is happy to have him in the company, for they are about to enter dangerous territory, the Enchanted Ground. With swords drawn, Great-heart walks in front, Valiant-for-truth behind "lest peradventure some fiend or dragon or giant or thief should fall upon their rear." Encouraged by Great-heart, they make "pretty good shift to wag along" even though mist and darkness descend upon them. There is much "grunting and puffing and sighing" as they plod along. "While one tumbleth over a bush, another sticks fast in the dirt; and the children, some of them lost their shoes in the mire." Coming to a pleasant arbor furnished with benches and couches, the weary Pilgrims are tempted to stop, but Great-heart warns them against this place, called Slothful's Friend, set up to entice Pilgrims to sit down and fall into a deep sleep from which they would never awaken.

Leading the procession in the dark, Great-heart comes to a place where he is uncertain which way to go. Having "struck a light (for he never goes out without his tinder-box)," he draws from his pocket a "book, or map, which bids him be careful in this place to turn to the right-hand way." It is well that he checked the map. Otherwise, the party would have taken another path leading to a pit, "none knows how deep, full of nothing but mud, there made on purpose to destroy the Pilgrims." As the party emerges from the Enchanted Ground, the wind comes up, dispelling the fog and mist, and they see ahead, making "a solemn noise," a man on his knees, with hands and eyes lifted up, "and speaking, as they thought to one that was above." He turns out to be Stand-fast, "a right good Pilgrim," and an old friend of Honest. They exchange stories about their adventures.

The most interesting of Stand-fast's concerned his meeting with a woman in the Enchanted Ground. Madam Bubble by name, she is a "tall comely dame, something of a swarthy complexion," is dressed attractively, and talks smoothly, ending every sentence with a smile. She carries a great purse at her side, filled with money, and often reaches into it to finger her gold and silver coins. In certain places and to certain persons, she scatters her gold like dust. She loves feasting and "to be sought after, spoken well of, and to lie in the bosoms of men. She is never weary of commending her commodities."

Seeing Stand-fast struggling along, Madam Bubble greets him, talks with him, and soon offers him "three things, to wit, her body, her purse, and her bed.... 'I am the Mistress of the World, and men are made happy by me.' " Though "a-weary and sleepy... and as poor as a howlet [owlet]," Stand-fast repulses her advances once, twice, many times, but still she follows him with inducements and enticements. Becoming angry, Stand-fast takes to his heels, falls on his knees, raises up his hands, lifts up his eyes, and prays to God to rescue him from this "witch."

All agree that she is a witch, a "bold and impudent slut [who] will talk with any man," and that Stand-fast did well to stand fast, which leads Great-heart to a bit of sermonizing: "Whoever doth lay his head down in her lap has as good lay it down upon that block over which the axe doth hang; and whoever lay their eyes upon her beauty are counted as the enemies of God [James 4:4; 1 John 2:15]....'Twas she that set Absalom against his father, and Jeroboam against his master. 'Twas she that persuaded Judas to sell his Lord, and that prevailed with Demas to forsake the godly Pilgrim's life.... She makes variance betwixt rulers and subjects, betwixt parents and children, 'twixt neighbor and neighbor, 'twixt a man and his wife, 'twixt a man and himself, 'twixt the flesh and the heart." With this, the Pilgrims begin to sing:

What danger is the Pilgrim in,
How many are his foes,
How many ways there are to sin,
No living mortal knows.
Some of the ditch shy are, yet can
Lie tumbling in the mire;
Some, though they shun the frying-pan,
Do leap into the fire.

Stand-fast joins Christiana's party, and now they are sixteen as they come into the Land of Beulah, "where the sun shineth night and day," as it did in Christian's time. Resting here a while, they are invited to help themselves to the luscious fruits and all else growing in the Lord's orchards, gardens, and vineyards. Among other things, they gather "camphire, with spikenard and saffron, calamus and cinnamon, with all its trees of frankincense, myrrh, and aloes, with all chief spices." With these, they "perfume" the chambers in the guest house where they are staying, and also use them to anoint their bodies against the time when they will be called to cross the Dark River. Altogether, Beulah Land is, quite literally, a divine spot, though there is so much ringing of bells, sounding of trumpets, and singing of angels that the Pilgrims can get no sleep. But they do not mind this, for they feel as fresh at all times as if they had not missed a wink of sleep.

One day there is a report in town that a messenger has arrived from the Celestial City bringing a note to Christiana, who hastily opens the message and reads: "Hail, good woman, I bring thee tidings that the Master calleth for thee and expecteth that thou shouldest stand in his presence, in clothes of immortality, within this ten days."

As Christiana prepares to depart, she speaks to all in the company, wishing them well, being escorted by them and everybody in town to the Dark River, the far bank of which is crowded with horses and chariots filled with Shining Ones. Wading into the stream, Christiana waves farewell to her friends and is soon whisked away in a chariot to the Celestial Gate.

The next to be summoned is Ready-to-halt, who throws away his crutches as he enters the river and cries out: "Welcome, life." Then follows Mr. Feeble-mind, who bequeathes his mind to Mr. Valiant with the request that he bury it in a dunghill, for it is of no use to anybody. Then, in turn, everybody is summoned to come over except Christiana's four sons and their young brides. These are temporarily left behind to propagate "for the increase of the Church in that place where they were for a time."

With this, the story ends. The author-dreamer does not give us the slightest glimpse of anything beyond the Celestial Gate – not even the picture offered in Part I of Christian and Hopeful joining the angels parading the gold-paved streets in the jewel-encrusted city, strumming their golden harps and singing.

Commentary

Nothing much exciting happens on the Celestial Mountains, but two things are of note. First, it appears that a palace had been built on the mountains since Christian's visit; he and Hopeful had been entertained in tents, which would seem to be more in the shepherdic tradition and manner of life. Second, Mercy covets a marvelous mirror in the palace, saying that she must have it if she is to avoid having a miscarriage. It is legendary that pregnant women have strange desires. Not wishing to have on their hands a miscarried Mercy, the shepherds happily present her with the looking glass which, held one way, shows the features of the person looking into it but, held another way, shows the image of Christ with a crown of thorns on his head and holes in his hands, feet, and side. The glass, "one of a thousand," is the Bible, which prevents Mercy's miscarriage.

The "book, or map," that Great-heart uses in guiding Christiana's party safely across the dangerous Enchanted Ground is another symbol of the Bible, and keeps the Pilgrims from taking a wrong turn in the dark and falling into a deep pit which would have trapped them all.

Stand-fast's account of his meeting with Madam Bubble in the Enchanted Ground and his headlong flight from her is graphic and entertaining in its details. Madam Bubble with her physical charms and great purse filled with gold which she scatters like dust to her favorites is Bunyan's personification of all that is alluring but ephemeral in the world, things that burst like a soap bubble. The Madam is so intent on seducing Stand-fast that he escapes, not by standing fast, but running away and falling on his knees in desperately pleading with God to rescue him from the "witch.... a bold and impudent slut," such a one as had seduced Absalom, Jeroboam, and Judas in ancient days. The song the Pilgrims sing to celebrate Stand-fast's rescue is one of Bunyan's better jingles.

Beulah Land, in this second part of the book, differs somewhat from the way Christian and Hopeful saw it. It now appears to be a sort of receiving station for those Heaven bound. While enjoying the delicacies from the Lord's orchards, gardens, and vineyards, Pilgrims wait here until each is personally summoned to advance to the Celestial Gate. Christiana is the first to be summoned and told to be ready within ten days. Mr. Ready-to-halt is the next to be called, then Mr. Feeble-mind, followed by Mr. Despondency and his daughter Much-afraid, and then by Old Honest.

The order here is symbolic: the handicapped should be helped first. In the end, all but Christiana's four sons and their wives go over the Dark River and are whisked up to the Pearly Gates. But the author offers us no glimpse into the heavenly Jerusalem the Pilgrims had struggled so hard to attain. He does not even show us Christian and Christiana embracing. Excusing himself for this, Bunyan concludes his book with this paragraph: "Shall it be my lot to go that way again, I may give... an account of what I here am silent about...."

REVIEW QUESTIONS AND ESSAY TOPICS

1. A Bunyan scholar has written: "Christian made a pilgrimage; Christiana went on a walking tour." What was the writer driving at?

2. Review the scene of Christiana's departure from the City of Destruction for the Celestial City. How does it differ from Christian's departure? What led her to a final decision?

3. What is your analysis of Mercy as a character? What purpose does she serve in the story?

4. How is Great-heart introduced into the story, and what does he symbolize?

5. What was the "universal pill" which Mr. Skill, the ancient physician, concocted at Palace Beautiful for curing Matthew of the "gripes" he got from eating green plums out of Satan's orchard? What is Bunyan's point in elaborating on this incident?

6. Explain the author's account of the reason why Christian's and Christiana's parties experience such very different things in the

Valley of Humiliation? Christian found it a place of terror; Mercy, the pleasantest place she had ever seen.

7. Review the scene at Vanity Fair and tell why the town seems to be so much improved since Christian passed through and Faithful was put to death there, being burned at the stake.

8. For what reason, in your opinion, does Bunyan introduce and make so much of such characters as Mr. Feeble-mind and Mr. Ready-to-halt, Mr. Despondency and his daughter Much-afraid?

9. Why is it, do you suppose, that the Holy Way, the King's highway to the heavenly Jerusalem, is so beset with fiends, devils, monsters, and malignant giants? Could there be a giant who was benign? Or is a "good" giant symbolically unfeasible? Look up the word "hagiology."

10. What interest, if any, has *The Pilgrim's Progress* for the modern reader? Be explicit in supporting whatever view you have.

Selected Bibliography

Biography (not listed alphabetically, but in the order of recommendation)

WINSLOW, OLA ELIZABETH. *John Bunyan.* New York, 1961. Scholarly, well conceived, and well written, this is perhaps the best biography for the general reader. The chapter of "The Pilgrim's Progress, 1678," is particulary useful.

TALON, HENRI. *John Bunyan: The Man and His Works.* London, 1951. See particularly the long chapter on "The Pilgrim's Progress," dealing with plot, symbolism, analysis of characters, etc.

BRITTAIN, VERA. *Valiant Pilgrim: The Story of John Bunyan and Puritan England.*

WHAREY, JAMES BLANTON. *Bunyan: "The Pilgrim's Progress"* (second revised edition by ROGER SHARROCK). Oxford and New York, 1960. Valuable notes on the changes made in the many editions of *The Pilgrim's Progress.*

TINDALL, W. YORK. *John Bunyan, Mechanick Preacher.* New York, 1934.

BROWN, JOHN. *Bunyan, His Life, Times and Works* (revised ed.). London, 1928. The standard and what might be called the "official" biography; because of voluminous minute detail, it is rather heavy going.

Interesting References

COCKETT, C. B. *Bunyan's England.* London, 1928.

FIRTH, CHARLES HARDING. "John Bunyan" in *Essays Historical and Literary.* Oxford, 1938.

FROUDE, J. A. *John Bunyan.* London, 1880.

GOLDER, HAROLD. "John Bunyan's Hypocrisy" in *North American Review,* Vol. 223, 1926.

HARRISON, G. B. *John Bunyan, a Study in Personality.* London, 1928.

KELMAN, JOHN. *The Road, a Study of John Bunyan's "Pilgrim's Progress."* London, 1917.

LEAVIS, F. R. "Bunyan in Modern Eyes," essay in *The Common Pursuit.* London, 1952.

MILLER, PERRY. "John Bunyan's *Pilgrim's Progress*" in *Classics of Religious Devotion.* Boston, 1950.

NOYES, ALFRED. "Bunyan—a Revaluation," in *Bookman,* Vol. 75, Oct., 1928.

SHAW, GEORGE BERNARD. *Dramatic Opinions and Essays.* London, 1907.

NOTES

NOTES